SECOND EDITION

Writing English

A Composition Text in English as a Foreign Language

Janet Ross
Ball State University

Gladys Doty
University of Colorado

HARPER & ROW, Publishers
New York, Evanston, San Francisco, London

Sponsoring Editor: *George J. Telecki*
Project Editor: *Elizabeth Dilernia*
Designer: *Frances Torbert Tilley*
Production Supervisor: *Will Jomarrón*

WRITING ENGLISH: *A Composition Text in English as a Foreign Language,* Second Edition

Library of Congress Cataloging in Publication Data
Ross, Janet.
   Writing English.
   Includes index.
   1. English language—Text-books for foreigners.
I. Doty, Gladys G., joint author. II. Title.
PE1128.R69 1975   428'.2'4   74-31998
ISBN 0-06-045591-8

Contents

Preface   ix

A Note to Students and Instructors on the Use of the Book   xii

PART ONE   Writing in Grammatical Patterns   1

LESSON   1   Identifying Syntactic Patterns   3
Basic Affirmative, Negative, and Interrogative
Sentence Patterns; Devices for Indicating Syntactic
Relationships

LESSON   2   Marking Nouns   18
Use and Omission of Articles; Other Markers of
Count and Non-Count Nouns

LESSON   3   Expressing Time: Verbs and Adverbs   29
Present, Past, and Future Time Expressions;
Continuous Forms; Two-Word Verbs and Verbs
with Prepositional Phrases

LESSON   4   Expressing Relationships in Time   40
Perfect Verb Forms; Positions of Adverbs

LESSON 5 Describing with Adjectivals and Passive Forms 55
Adjectives and Phrases as Modifiers of Nouns,
Qualifiers of Adjectives; Uses of the Passive
Voice

LESSON 6 Describing with Relative Clauses and Verbals 65
Clauses and Reductions of Clauses as Modifiers
of Nouns

LESSON 7 Using Verbals and Clauses as Nouns: Showing
Relationships Between Clauses and Sentences 76
Verbals as Subjects and Objects, Adverbial
Structures; Subordinators and Sentence
Connectors

LESSON 8 Expressing Attitudes with Modals: A Further Word
on Verbals 90
Uses of Modal Auxiliaries; Infinitives as Adverbials
and as Complements of Adjectives

PART TWO Writing in Rhetorical Patterns 101

LESSON 9 Writing the Longer Composition 103
An Overview

LESSON 10 Choosing a Subject and Stating It Clearly 113
How the Author and Reader Affect the Choice and
the Statement

LESSON 11 Developing and Supporting Ideas 125
Details, Facts, Figures, Examples, Illustration,
Quotation

LESSON 12 Organizing the Composition 144
Time Order, Space Order, Topical Order

LESSON 13 Making Ideas Clear 162
Definition, Comparison, Contrast, Explanation,
Restatement

LESSON 14 Organizing the Composition   176
           Cause-Effect Order; Problem-Solution Order

LESSON 15 Organizing the Composition   188
           Deductive and Inductive Order; Writing Essay
           Examinations

LESSON 16 Writing the Library Research Paper   202
           Locating Suitable Material; Taking Notes;
           Integrating the Material into Your Own
           Composition; Giving Credit for Material Taken
           from Others

APPENDIX   227

I. Charts of Selected Grammatical Points   229
   A. Nouns   229
   B. Verbs   232
   C. Prepositions   243
   D. Subordinators and Conjunctions   246

II. Conventions in the Mechanics of Writing   249
   A. Rules for Punctuation   249
   B. Rules for Capitalization   256
   C. Forms for Acknowledging Borrowed Material and Ideas   258
   D. Abbreviations   259

INDEX   261

Preface

Writing English is a textbook in written composition for intermediate or advanced students of English as a foreign language. This second edition incorporates changes that we feel will make it more effective in providing a review of grammar and helping students write paragraphs and longer compositions.

Before the ink is dry on the final page of any manuscript, authors have the feeling that they would make certain changes if they were doing it over. Since writing the first edition of *Writing English*, we have had not only the experience of using the book ourselves, but the additional benefit of suggestions from others who have used it. Through teaching classes in composition to foreign students we have also developed new techniques that we have found effective. Research on language and language learning has also modified our thinking, and this in turn has influenced our selection of classroom activities designed to help students write correctly and with greater enthusiasm and confidence.

Writing involves the use of correct grammatical patterns to express ideas clearly. It also involves using various rhetorical devices to pinpoint ideas and to support, develop, or clarify them.

Expressing ideas in any language is a matter of options. Although certain points of grammar are fixed, almost any idea can be phrased in a number of ways at the sentence level. Any longer message (composition, term paper, thesis, or even the answer to an examination question) can make use of varied methods of development and organization. Cultures differ in the means they use to present and amplify ideas. The purpose of this textbook is to show students what options are available to the writer and what rules of writing he or she must conform to when writing in English.

In overall organization the book moves from a primary focus on grammatical patterns to a primary focus on rhetorical ones. Part One provides a review of basic grammatical patterns but also illustrates in example passages not only the grammatical points being discussed but the rhetorical devices by which the ideas are presented to the attention of the reader. The first lesson provides a general review of the basic syntactic structure of an English sentence. Subsequent lessons have been arranged so that matters which seem to cause the most difficulty for the heterogeneous class in English as a foreign language are presented first. Information about grammatical principles has been made more succinct, and many of the lists and charts that appeared in the text of the first edition have been placed in the appendix. Most of the sentence structure exercises have been put into a rhetorical framework. Longer composition assignments at the end of each lesson call for use of the patterns practiced in the lesson. They also give the student a chance to gain some fluency in writing connected discourse before he or she starts a formal study of rhetorical principles. The compositions in this part are "guided" in that an organizational pattern is provided for the student, who is led to use the structures practiced in the preceding sentence and paragraph exercises.

Part Two places major stress on rhetorical devices. The theory of American rhetoric is discussed in more detail than in the first edition so that students can better understand what rhetoric is and how a study of it will help them in their writing. This section calls attention to culture-bound rhetorical differences. Many examples of good writing have been introduced, with analysis of those samples that will help the student learn the kinds of ways available for developing an idea and selecting the appropriate means of handling a given subject. Added features are the suggestions in Lesson 15 for writing answers to essay-type examination questions and the discussion in Lesson 16 of the procedure to follow in writing a paper based on library research.

This book emphasizes the importance of the writer's being aware of the reader. What the writer says and how it is stated depend upon what the reader already knows, where his or her interests lie, and what his or her attitudes are. Such an awareness affects vocabulary, sentence structure and length, ways in which a point is developed, and the overall organization. Writing for a reader also increases motivation of the writer. Teachers are often astonished by the fluency of student writing after a heated class discussion. Thus we furnish a variety of topics for compositions and encourage exchange of ideas. If students are asked to react to each other's writing, it is easier for them to realize when they need to define terms more clearly, give more detailed explanation, or state the relationship between ideas more explicitly.

We wish to thank both instructors and students who have used this book and have given suggestions for revisions. We particularly want to thank Nan James for her typing of the manuscript and for her constructive comments.

Janet Ross
Gladys Doty

A Note to Students and Instructors on the Use of the Book

Classes in English for foreign students in American schools are usually made up of students with varying degrees of proficiency in writing English and with different areas of weakness in their knowledge of English structure. This book is designed with these differences in mind. Few classes may want to go through the book from Lesson 1 to the end, with every student doing every exercise. Instead, the book may be used in one of the following ways.

Classes may proceed from Lesson 1, with instructors and students selecting exercises according to the needs of the class as a whole, or of the individual student. Students may then write the controlled composition at the end of each lesson and progress lesson by lesson to the study of rhetoric and the freer composition assignments in Part Two. Other classes, perhaps those having more familiarity with English structure, may wish to read the illustrative passages for study in each lesson in Part One and go directly to the controlled composition, returning to such exercises as seem indicated by errors in grammatical structure made in the composition. Not all students may need the same exercises. A third alternative for more advanced classes is to begin with the rhetoric and relatively unstructured composition assignments in Part Two, reviewing exercises in Part One on points of grammatical structure as needed.

PART ONE
Writing
in Grammatical Patterns

Identifying Syntactic Patterns

Basic Affirmative, Negative, and Interrogative Sentence Patterns; Devices for Indicating Syntactic Relationships

In order to write good English sentences one must observe the principles of sentence construction. The basic elements of a sentence are the verb and the nouns that stand in relation to it as subjects, objects, or complements, and occasionally as adverbials. Every sentence has as its basis a verb and at least one noun or pronoun as subject. In English the relationship between the verb and the nouns, as well as between other parts of a sentence, is expressed largely by word order, although word endings and the use of words such as prepositions for relational markers are important also. The verb controls the primary noun–verb patterns. It determines the number of basic elements in the sentence, each of which occupies a given position. In speaking, we often omit the verb or the subject and verb, particularly in answering questions. In writing expository communication, they are generally stated.

This introductory lesson gives you practice in identifying the basic sentence elements and reviews the subject–verb–complement patterns of English. Elementary exercises are provided for those who need basic review. There are more advanced exercises for those who have mastered the elementary principles and want to explore ways of producing more elaborate sentences. After completing Exercise 1, students and instructors may decide which exercises are appropriate for an individual student.

PASSAGE FOR STUDY

Civilization's Debt to Books

Bookmaking began many years ago. Printing made bookmaking easier, and printing thus quietly revolutionized the world. Because of printing, reading has become widespread, and the accumulated knowledge of the past is now in the hands of all the people rather than just a few. The literate man learns of things that are remote from him in time and space. The illiterate man might consider many of these things impossibilites. Some books drift casually through our lives, but some permanently affect what we think, what we are, and what we do. A writer goes beneath the surface of the subject he writes about. Thus he brings us new insights. Books are the immortality of man.

▶ Exercise 1

In the passage "Civilization's Debt to Books," the sentences follow the subject–verb and subject–verb–complement patterns that are basic in English. To test your knowledge of these patterns and your ability to distinguish them, study the passage. Then find and write sentences from the passage illustrating each of the following patterns. Label the subjects, verbs, objects, complements, and adverbials. The first one is done for you.

1. A sentence with a subject–verb–adverbial pattern:

    S   V   ADV

    Bookmaking began many years ago.

2. A sentence with a subject–verb–object pattern
3. A sentence with a subject–verb–indirect object–object pattern
4. A sentence with a subject–verb–object–objective complement (adjective) pattern
5. A sentence with a subject–linking verb–subjective complement (adjective) pattern

6. A sentence with a subject–*be*–subjective complement (noun) pattern

When you have finished, check your answers with the patterns which follow.

Basic Sentence Patterns

The basic subject–verb–object or complement patterns of English are summarized as follows.

PATTERN 1: *Subject–Verb* (Adverbial)

    S   V   ADV

Bookmaking began many years ago.

Verbs that follow this pattern are called intransitive. Although the adverb may not be a basic part of this subject–verb pattern, some sentences with intransitive verbs need adverbs or adverbial phrases to make the idea complete.

PATTERN 2: *Subject–Verb–Object*

    S   V   O

Printing revolutionized the world.

Verbs that are followed by an object are called transitive.

PATTERN 3: *Subject–Verb–Indirect Object–Object*

    S   V   IO   O

He brings us new insights.

Verbs in this pattern are also transitive. Common verbs that can be used with an indirect object are:

bring	find	grant	paint	send	tell
draw	give	leave	sell	show	write

PATTERN 4: *Subject–Verb–Object–Objective Complement* (Noun or Adjective)

       s   o   v   oc (ADJ)
a. Printing made bookmaking easier.

                  s   v   o
b. The illiterate man considers many of these things
oc (N)
impossibilities.

Transitive verbs are also used in this pattern. The complement, which is a noun or adjective, is called the objective complement because it refers to the object. Verbs commonly used with an objective complement are:

believe	choose	elect	make	think	want
call	consider	fine	suppose	vote	

All of these verbs except *choose, elect,* and *vote* can be used with an adjective after the noun.

PATTERN 5: *Subject–Linking Verb–Subjective Complement* (Noun or Adjective)

      s   v   c (ADJ)
a. Books have become widespread.

      s   v   c (N)
b. This book became a best seller.

A linking verb joins a subject with a subjective complement (noun or adjective) that refers to the subject. Linking verbs commonly used with adjectives are:

appear,	grow	sound
look, seem	prove	taste
become	remain	turn
feel	smell	

Become and *remain* may be used with nouns as complements.

PATTERN 6: *Subject–be–Complement* (Noun, Adjective, or Adverbial of Location)

    s   v   c (N)
a. Books are the immortality of man.

    s   v   c (ADJ)
b. Books are informative.

    s   v   c (ADV)
c. Books are everywhere.

Elementary Review Writing Exercises

Exercises 2 through 9 provide a review of the basic sentence patterns in simple writing exercises. You may wish to do some or all of them, or go on to Exercise 10, depending on your familiarity with the material.

▶ Exercise 2

The opening sentence of a paragraph often states the general topic of the paragraph. In the passage on books at the beginning of the lesson, the topic sentence is the second: "Printing made bookmaking easier, and printing thus quietly revolutionized the world."

A. Write a short paragraph (five or six sentences) about activities that you do every day. Use as the first sentence of your paragraph the topic sentence:

There are some things that I do every day during the school year.

Develop it by giving examples. Use simple s–v or s–v–o patterns (Sentence Patterns 1 and 2 in Exercise 1, above).

Examples
I get up at seven o'clock.
I eat breakfast at 7:30.

Add a concluding sentence to express your attitude toward this routine.

B. Change your topic sentence to:

There are some things that a student does every day during the school year.

Develop it in a similar fashion. Note the change in the verb form when the subject is *he, she,* or *it* (third person singular).

Examples
He *gets* up at seven o'clock.
He *takes* a shower before breakfast.

Negative Patterns

A. Sentences with verbs except *be* form the negative by using *does not* or *do not* (past tense: *did not*) as follows:

Singular: This book *does not interest* me.
Plural: These books *do not interest* me.
Past tense: This book (these books) *did not interest* me.

Compare the affirmative patterns:

This book *interests* me.
These books *interest* me.
This book *interested* me.

B. Sentences with the verb *be* form the negative merely by putting *not* after the verb.

This book *is not* mine.

▶ **Exercise 3**

A. Choose one of these topic sentences for the opening sentence of a paragraph:

My roommate (friend) is always trying to save money.
My roommate (friend) is a very peculiar fellow (girl).

My brother (sister) is very different from me.

My roommate (friend) is very resourceful (clever, intelligent).

Complete the paragraph by adding s–v or s–v–o pattern sentences to give examples that support your opinion about him. Make some of your sentences negative.

Example
My roommate is always trying to save money. He does his own laundry. He cuts his own hair. He does not smoke. He never asks a girl for a date.

Keep your sentences simple. Do not try to write structures you are unsure of.

B. Change the subject to the plural.

Example
My friends in the dormitory, my brothers and sisters, my classmates. . . .

Add sentences as before. Make some of them negative. Note changes in verbs.

Examples
My friends *study* all night and *sleep* all day.
They *do not like* to listen to my record player.

▶ **Exercise 4.**

Note Sentence Pattern 3: *Subject–Verb–Indirect Object–Object*. For practice in using this pattern with an indirect object, write a paragraph of a few sentences telling what someone did for you or gave to you on some occasion when you went to a new place, or went on a trip somewhere. Begin with a topic sentence like one of the following (you may want to change it a bit to suit the situation you are writing about):

Many people (nobody) helped me when I arrived in (city).

The people in (city) helped me when I arrived to study at the university.

Many people helped me plan my trip to (country).

In your paragraph you may want to mention some of the following:

a policeman	my parents	a scholarship commission
a travel agent	a taxi driver	a man passing by
the consulate	the airlines clerk	the hotel desk clerk

Example
A man in the airport showed me the airport limousine.

Add a concluding sentence to your paragraph, such as:

Without their help my trip (visit) would have been much more difficult.

Remember that most verbs add *–ed* to form the past tense. For irregular verbs see the Appendix, pp. 232–233.

▶ **Exercise 5**

Note Sentence Pattern 4: *Subject–Verb–Object–Objective Complement.* For practice in using this pattern, write A or B.

A. Write a paragraph of a few sentences telling about the meeting of a club or organization you belong to. Begin with a topic sentence such as:

The International Student Club (or other organization) conducted some important business last week.

Add a direct object and an objective complement to at least four of the following and include them in your paragraph to explain what happened at the meeting.

Example
The students chose _____.
The students chose Walter the leader.

1. The president (chairman, members, group, etc.) chose _____.
2. The group (president, majority, etc.) considered _____.
3. The class (chairman, president) appointed _____.
4. The members elected _____.
5. The organization made _____.
6. A majority voted _____.

B. Write a paragraph in which you contrast your opinions of several movie stars, radio or TV personalities, or characters in history. Use the Subject–Verb–Object–Objective Complement pattern in at least four sentences. Suggested topic sentences with ideas for development are:

Although I like some TV performers, others bore (outrage, annoy) me. I consider _____ the best musical entertainer. He (she) . . .

There are certain historical figures whom I admire tremendously. Although Alexander the Great has always appeared very temperamental, I think he would be fun to talk to some evening. I would ask him if he purposely set fire to Persepolis, but maybe he would consider the question impertinent . . .

Develop the paragraph by telling which persons you might consider to be some of the following:

odd	fortunate	disappointing	weak
wicked	arrogant	fascinating	resourceful
kind	charming	adventurous	boring
wise	mysterious	honorable	unusual
comical	foolish	extraordinary	offensive

▶ **Exercise 6**

Note Sentence Pattern 5: *Subject–Linking Verb–Subjective Complement* (Noun or Adjective). For practice in this pattern write on A or B.

A. Use the following idea as your topic sentence:

People I have known (or have read about) have entered (or will enter) many different lines of work.

Develop the idea by writing sentences to tell who became (or will become) five of the following. When possible, give the names of persons whom you know or about whom you have read.

a nurse	a doctor	a banker	a businessman
an actor	an author	a secretary	a housewife
a farmer	a teacher	a painter	a lawyer

B. Use the following as your topic sentence:

I enjoyed (did not enjoy) a party I attended last week.

Develop the idea by writing sentences to tell how something *looked, appeared, seemed, sounded, tasted,* or *smelled.*

Example
The soup smelled wonderful and tasted even better.

Question Patterns

A. Sentences with verbs except *be* are turned into questions by the use of *does (do, did)* as follows:

Statement: This book *interests* me.
Question:

        Singular: *Does* this book *interest* you?
        Plural: *Do* these books *interest* you?
        Past: *Did* this (these) book (books) *interest* you?

B. Sentences with *be* are turned into questions as follows:

Is the book on the table?
Are you *going?*

▶ **Exercise 7**

Each member of the class will think of a famous person that you all have read about. Write a paragraph beginning:

I am trying to guess who it is you are thinking of.

Add ten questions you might ask in trying to guess who the person is.

Examples
Is he living?
Is the person a man?
Does (Did) he live in the Western Hemisphere?
Does (Did) he play a role in politics?

In class you will read your paragraph to a class member. He will answer each question by saying "Yes" or "No." Perhaps you can guess who it is that your classmate is thinking of before you have finished reading your paragraph.

Variations of Patterns with Be

In variations of Sentence Pattern 6 with *be*, the words *it* or *there* may stand in the subject position as follows:

PATTERN 6a: There–v–n

There	v	n	(ADV)
There	is	a building	on the corner.
There	are	many people	in the city.

The true subject of the sentence in this pattern is the noun following the verb. Note that it governs the form of the verb. One could also say, "A building is on the corner." While *be* is the verb commonly used in this pattern, other verbs sometimes used are *appear, come, exist, happen, live, occur, seem,* and *sit.*

There *appeared* a face at the window.
There *comes* a time when we must go.

PATTERN 6b: It–v   or   It–be–n (ADJ)

It	v	n (ADJ)
It	is raining.	
It	is	cold.
It	is	ten o'clock.

Expressions like this are used to indicate time or weather. *It* in such sentences has no meaning, but is used to fill the subject position in the sentence.

PATTERN 6c: It–be–ADJ–*Clause* (Phrase)

It	*be*	ADJ	*Clause* (Phrase)
It	is	important	that you come.
It	is	useless	to protest.

Sentences like this represent a transposition or "transformation" of the sentence elements for emphasis. This pattern is sometimes called the *it* transform and will be studied more fully in later lessons.

▶ **Exercise 8**

The pattern with *There is* is used to make assertions about the general appearance of something, or general conditions.

Example
There are fifty stars and thirteen stripes in the flag of the United States of America. There is a stripe for each of the thirteen original states. In a law passed by Congress in 1818 there is a provision for the addition of a new star whenever a new state is added to the union. Thus there have been changes in the flag throughout the history of the country.

Note that in this short paragraph the topic sentence that the paragraph develops is stated at the end.

Write a few sentences making assertions that you consider to be true about the appearance or general nature of something with which you are familiar. Introduce a number of your sentences by *there is* or *there are*. Put the topic sentence at the beginning or at the end.

Example
There are many canals in the Netherlands. There are also many windmills there. . . . These things are typical of the scenery of my country. (topic sentence at the end)

▶ **Exercise 9**

Review the basic patterns presented in this lesson. One of the basic elements in each of the following sentences makes the meaning improbable or nonsensical. Replace the inappropriate element with an appropriate one. Then identify the basic pattern of the sentence by the pattern numbers used in this lesson.

1. The young man gave his girlfriend a fierce man-eating tiger.
2. Silence made Churchill a great speaker.
3. The lovely gift was refused with pleasure.
4. When you cultivate ideas you must deny them time to grow.
5. The raucous singers sound soothing.
6. John's frivolous wife became the chairman of the company's Board of Directors.

Variations and Rearrangements of Basic Sentence Patterns

The basic sentence pattern contains one subject, verb, and object or complement. However, elements may be coordinated or repeated, the sentence may be transposed, or elements may interrupt the s–v–o pattern. The passage and exercises that follow illustrate some of these modifications.

More Advanced Exercises

PASSAGE FOR STUDY

The Changing Sea[1]

(1) For the sea as a whole, the alternation of day and night, the passage of the seasons, the procession of the years are lost in its vastness, obliterated in its own changeless eternity. (2) But the surface waters are different. (3) The face of the sea is always changing. (4) Crossed by colors, lights, and moving shadows, sparkling in the sun, mysterious in the twilight, its aspects and the moods vary hour by hour. (5) The surface waters move with

---

[1] Rachel Carson, *The Sea Around Us,* pp. 28–29. Copyright © 1950, 1951, 1961 by Rachel Carson. Reprinted by permission of Oxford University Press, Inc.

the tides, stir to the breath of the winds, and rise and fall to the endless, hurrying forms of the waves. (6) Most of all, they change with the advance of the seasons. (7) Spring moves over the temperate lands of our Northern Hemisphere in a tide of new life, of pushing green shoots and unfolding buds, all its mysteries and meanings symbolized in the northward migration of the birds, the awakening of sluggish amphibian life as the chorus of frogs rises again from the wet lands, the different sound of the wind which stirs the young leaves where a month ago it rattled bare branches. (8) These things we associate with the land, and it is easy to suppose that at sea there could be no such feeling of advancing spring. (9) But the signs are there, and seen with understanding eye, they bring the same magical sense of awakening.

▶ **Exercise 10**

Note how Rachel Carson, author of "The Changing Sea," repeats a sentence element in many of the sentences in order to make the picture vivid in the mind of the reader. For example, sentence 1 has more than one subject and more than one verb plus modifier. The basic s–v sentence pattern is expanded to s,s,s–v,v. In sentence 5 the verb element is repeated, and all three of the verbs are followed by a prepositional phrase. Sentence 7 displays the building up of a series of modifiers of nouns and modifiers of verbs. Such repetition of the same structure is called parallel (or coordinate) structure.

Answer these questions on the passage:

1. Identify the repeated sentence elements in sentence 1 by writing them and labeling them as s, v.
2. List the repeated parallel modifiers in sentence 4. What do they modify?
3. List the parallel adverbials in sentence 7 that modify the verb *moves*.
4. What other example of parallel structure do you find in sentence 7? On what preposition do they all depend?
5. In sentence 7 what is the function of the word *symbolized*?
6. In sentence 8 the word *it* in the expression "it is easy to suppose" is a subject filler, sometimes called a dummy subject. See Sen-

tence Pattern 6c. What is the true subject of the sentence? That is, what is it that is "easy"?

▶ Exercise 11

In five or six sentences describe something in or near your home, such as the living room on the morning after a party, the garden in the fall, a village in the rain. Or describe a busy public place at the rush hour: a bus or railway station, airport, hotel or market, or your campus before the first morning class. Or write a similar description telling how something sounded. Take a point of view toward your subject in the opening or the final sentence. In at least one sentence pile up subjects (the houses, the streets, the rooftops); in at least one sentence pile up verbs or verbs and modifiers (dripped with rivers of rain, were beaten by the vigorous downpour, and the like). Underline the repeated elements in your sentences.

Marking Nouns *Use and Omission of Articles; Other Markers of Count and Non-Count Nouns*

PASSAGE FOR STUDY

Adventure on the Colorado[1]

If you enjoy adventure, the delight of seeing something new along with a little bit of danger, you may go on a safari in Africa and face wild game, or view your native city from a parachute. Or you may prefer to experience the thrill of seeing the Grand Canyon of the Colorado River from a little boat.

Many oarsmen regard the Colorado as the roughest navigable river in the world. As it flows through the 285-mile long Grand Canyon, it drops 2,000 feet and contains more than 150 rapids. The current is so strong in a few of the rapids that it can peel a man like a banana, stripping off his pants, belt, shirt, and shoes in a few minutes. Few natural sounds on the planet are more intimidating than the thunder of this water.

The first man to travel through the Grand Canyon by river was Major John Wesley Powell, the one-armed explorer, who made the trip by rowboat in 1869. Tourists can now experience for themselves

---

[1] Facts taken from Robert Wallace, "Wooden Boats Plus Colorado River Equals Adventure," *Smithsonian,* vol. 5, no. 2 (May 1974), 37–43.

the things that impressed Powell, things that can be seen and heard in no other way. The trip begins some miles above the canyon and ends at Lake Mead, which is formed by Boulder Dam. A motorized barge makes the trip in eight or ten days, the passengers camping along the river bank at night. The barge can handle up to thirty people. But a small boat like Powell's carrying the oarsman-guide and two or three passengers takes a little less than three weeks. This is the way to see the river in its most awesome aspects.

The beginning of the trip is calm. The small boat moves slowly between limestone cliffs some 2,000 feet high. The view changes as it drifts toward a pure abstract sculpture made by the force of the water against the rock, or toward some high distant promontory green with pines. In some places the rock formations are the oldest in the world that are exposed to the sight of man. Their age is estimated at two billion years. Suddenly the calmness vanishes as you approach a rapid. The noise makes a man's chest vibrate like a drum. Caught in a whirlpool, the boat may spin with startling speed, or it may stand straight upward on its stern as it plunges into a hole.

Those who have taken such guided trips, however, claim that there is little problem of survival, as the danger of drowning is small. Though the boats often upset, they are built to be unsinkable, and the passengers are protected by life-jackets. In the most dangerous places the guides advise the passengers to get out and walk. Many people are so delighted with the trip that they want to take it a second time to experience once more the adventure of the water and the beauty of the canyon.

Count and Non-Count Nouns with Articles

In the passage you have just read, some of the nouns are preceded by the articles *a* or *the*. Others have no article before them. Note:

If you enjoy *adventure*
the delight of seeing something new
go on *a safari*
face *wild game*

The use or omission of articles is a difficult problem for those learning English as a foreign language, since many languages do not have markers of nouns, or mark them with articles according to a different system. In English the use or omission of the article depends on whether or not the noun indicates something that may be counted and whether or not it is definitized, as follows:

Count versus non-count

Nouns may indicate things that can be counted. Such things may be talked about in the plural, for example: *a man, two men; the idea, the ideas.* Non-count nouns indicate generalizations that may not be talked about in the plural, for example: *danger, excitement, adventure, beauty.* Such nouns are not preceded by the articles *a* or *the*.

Note that some non-count nouns may become count nouns. We may talk of our love for *adventure* (a generalization) or of *an adventure* (or two or three) that we had last week. Also, the meaning of a noun may change according to whether it is used as a count or non-count noun, for example: *a game* (a contest, a sport) and *game* (wild animals that one hunts). A list of non-count nouns may be found in the Appendix, pp. 230–232.

Indefinite versus definite

A noun may refer to an indefinite, unspecified thing, or to something definite. Non-definitized count nouns are marked in the singular in English by the indefinite article *a, an* (meaning one, any unspecified one). The plural has no marker unless a definite number is specified.

Example
   A book is on the table. (non-definitized singular count noun)
   Books bring pleasure to life. (non-definitized plural count noun)

Note that in "Adventure on the Colorado," pp. 18–19, the first time the motorized barge is referred to, it is indefinite: "*a* motorized barge." When it is mentioned again in the succeeding sentence, it is definitized: "*the* motorized barge." In the second reference it is *the* definite thing just mentioned.

Example
  The book is on the table.
  The books are on the table. (definitized count noun—the book or books you are talking about)

Non-count nouns may also be definitized by the article *the* when the definiteness is specified.

Example
  Books bring pleasure to life. (non-definitized non-count noun)
  He does not know *the pleasure of reading.* (definitized non-count noun)

The use of articles with count and non-count nouns is summarized in the chart that follows.

Summary of Uses of a *and* the *with Count and Non-Count Nouns*

	Count Nouns		Non-Count Nouns
			Singular
	Singular	*Plural*	*(no plural form)*
Nondefinitized	a book	books	beauty
Definitized	*the* book	*the* books	*the* beauty of nature

▶ **Exercise 1**

Study the uses and omission of *a* and *the* just given. Characterize the following nouns taken from the selection "Adventure on the Colorado" as count or non-count, singular or plural, indefinite or definite to account for the use of the article. The first two are done for you.

	Count/ Non-Count	Singular/ Plural	Definite/ Indefinite
Paragraph 1			
1. if you enjoy *adventure*	Non-count	Singular	Indefinite
2. the *delight* of seeing something new	Non-count	Singular	Definite
3. a *safari*			
4. *wild game*			
Paragraph 2			
5. the *current* is so strong			
6. it can peel a *man*			
7. *tourists* can now experience			
8. the *things* that impressed Powell			
9. *things* that can be seen and heard			
Paragraph 3			
10. exposed to the sight of *man*			
11. the *calmness* vanishes			
12. spin with startling *speed*			
Paragraph 4			
13. protected by *life-jackets*			
14. problem of *survival*			
15. to experience the *adventure* of the water			

▶ **Exercise 2**

Reread the passage "Adventure on the Colorado." Then write in complete sentences the answers to the following questions based on it. Pay particular attention to the use of articles. When you have finished, check your answers with the original. Did you use articles correctly? Check the spelling of unfamiliar words.

1. If you enjoy adventure, what are some things you can do?
2. How do many oarsmen regard the Colorado?

3. Who was the first man to travel through the Grand Canyon by river? How did he make the trip?
4. What can tourists now experience for themselves?
5. How long does the trip take by small boat?
6. What are some things you can see as the boat drifts between limestone cliffs?
7. How old are some of the rock formations?
8. What change takes place as you approach a rapid?
9. What may happen to the boat?
10. What do those who have taken the trip claim?
11. How are the passengers protected?
12. Why do some people want to take the trip a second time?

▶ **Exercise 3**

Assume you are taking a long trip by (name your means of transportation—plane, bus, car, train, foot, horseback, etc.) to a distant place. Write a paragraph beginning with the topic sentence:

I am packing for my trip to (place) by (means of transportation).

Add sentences telling which of the following you will include. Use markers of nouns when appropriate.

clothing	shaving lotion	radio	toothbrush
hat	makeup	scarves[2]	scissors
umbrella	razor	books	candy that
medicine	alarm clock	pen	you gave me

▶ **Exercise 4**

Begin a paragraph with one of these as the topic sentence:

There are some school subjects that I enjoy more than others.

I enjoy watching certain spectator sports.

There are many sports that I like to take part in.

Add a few sentences naming the subjects or sports you enjoy and telling why you enjoy or do not enjoy each one. Remember,

---

[2] A list of irregular plurals of nouns is found in the Appendix, pp. 229–230.

names of school subjects and sports are generalized. They are not used in the plural. What article—if any—will you use in most cases?

▶ **Exercise 5**

By using each in a sentence, show the difference in meaning between the following as count and non-count nouns. The first one is done for you.

1. a (the) force (an organized group)   1. force

   The office force gave the retiring secretary a gift. (count)
   He had to use *force* to open the door. (non-count)

2. a (the) company (a business   2. company
   establishment)
3. an (the) iron (for pressing clothes)   3. iron (metal)
4. an (the) honor (token of respect)   4. honor
5. the senses (means of perception)   5. sense (intelligence)
6. a (the) tea (party)   6. tea
7. a (the) work (composition)   7. work

▶ **Exercise 6**

A. In the selection "Adventure on the Colorado" note the distinction between "If you enjoy *adventure*" (paragraph 1) and "*the adventure* of the water" (last paragraph). The noun *adventure* is a non-count noun, but when it is definitized by a descriptive phrase ("of the water"), the definitization is signaled by *the*. Rewrite the following sentences making the italicized nouns definite by adding phrases to particularize them. The first one is done for you.

1. *Adventure* is exciting.

   I enjoy *the adventure* of traveling through the Grand Canyon by boat.

2. I enjoy *music*.
3. *Heroes* should get recognition. (Note the irregular plural *heroes*.)

4. Fiction is not always based on *fact*.
5. *Color* adds pleasure to life.
6. *People* are funny.
7. Many people thrive on *danger*.
8. *Beauty* should be enjoyed.

B. In the selection "Adventure on the Colorado" find four more examples of non-count nouns that are definitized.

Other Markers of Count and Non-Count Nouns

Nouns may be marked by words other than articles. Count nouns may be marked to indicate number, because they can be counted. Non-count nouns may be marked to indicate amount. Both may be marked to show possession. Note the examples from "Adventure on the Colorado":

many oarsmen (indefinite number)
his pants, belt, shirt (possession)
ten days (number)

Compare:

The current is so strong in a *few* of the rapids (a small number)
Few natural sounds . . . are more intimidating (almost no natural sounds)

Note how the meaning is changed if the article is omitted in the first sentence, or included in the second.

Compare also:

in *some* places (a limited number, not all)
some 2,000 feet (almost 2,000 feet)
some high distant promontory (an indefinite one)

These different meanings of *some* are indicated in speech by a difference in stress.

Compare:

> Sóme people like adventure. (Not all do.)
> Some péople came to visit us. (We do not indicate definitely who they were.)

In negative statements and in questions an indefinite amount or number is expressed by *any*—not *some*.

Compare:

> I have *some* money. (an indefinite amount)
> I do not have *any* money. (none)
> Do you have *any* money? (an unspecified amount)

Uses of markers of nouns other than articles are summarized in the table that follows.

Markers of Nouns:
Summary of Uses

	With Count Nouns			With Non-Count Nouns	
Indefinite Item	Definite Item	Indefinite Number	Definite Number	Indefinite Amount	Definite Amount
a	the	few[a,b]	no	little[b]	no
any	this,	a few[a,b]	all[a]	a little[b]	all
either	that	several[a]	every	some	
neither	these,	some[a]	one,	much	
	those[a]	many[a]	two, etc.	more,	
	his,	any	both[a]	most	
	her, etc.	more,			
	each	most[a]			
	another				

[a] These markers are used with plural count nouns.
[b] *Few* stresses a small number; *little* stresses small quantity. *A few* and *a little* do not stress small number or quantity.

▶ **Exercise 7**

This is an oral exercise. In a complete sentence each student will tell about the culture of his country by indicating in a general way the amount of something in each of the following groups that is found in the country. Use words like *few, a few, little, a little, many, much, some, no* to indicate amount.

Examples

feasts   There are *many feasts* during the holidays in _____ (country).

earthquakes   There are not *any earthquakes in* _____ (country).

                                              or

There are *no earthquakes* in _____ (country).

wild game	rainy days	colleges
wild animals	earthquakes	hospitals
beautiful birds	tornadoes	factories
insects	hot, dry weather	medical care
tax problems		spectacular scenery
traffic jams		mountains
economic depression		ocean beaches
divorces		rivers

▶ **Exercise 8**

Orally or in writing as your instructor directs, answer these questions about the rhetorical patterns in the selection "Adventure on the Colorado."

1. It was noted in Lesson 1 that a unit of expository writing centers on an idea that it expands or develops. The main idea of a paragraph may be stated in a *topic sentence*. The sentence that states the unifying idea of a longer essay is called the *thesis sentence*. The central purpose or thesis of the essay "Adventure on the Colorado" is suggested in the last sentence of the first paragraph. What is it? Is it a clear-cut thesis sentence?

2. What is the relation of the first sentence to the second? What similarity of idea does it have?

3. The paragraphs following the first one do not contain clear-cut topic sentences. Each paragraph has a central idea, however, that unifies it. Paragraph 2 describes the river itself. The description is the unifying element. What is the unifying idea of paragraph 3? Of paragraph 4?

4. The last paragraph is the conclusion. How does it restate the central idea that is indicated in the first paragraph?

Composition

Write a three-paragraph composition about something a visitor to your country might enjoy doing or enjoy seeing. In your introductory paragraph take a point of view about your subject in a topic sentence that will appear at the end of the paragraph. Introduce the paragraph by giving alternative points of view, or alternative things the visitor might see or do, as in the first paragraph of "Adventure on the Colorado."

In the second paragraph answer these questions:

1. What are the general characteristics (or some unusual characteristic) of the place you are going to describe?
2. Where is it located?
3. Who first discovered it, or built it, or used it, or took a trip to it?
4. Why will visitors enjoy it today?

In paragraph 3 tell some of the specific things or features a person will see or things he will do when he visits this place. Use markers such as *some, any, few, a few,* and so on, to characterize amounts or qualities. End with a concluding or summary statement.

When the composition is finished, check your use of *a* and *the* as markers of nouns. Be able to defend your use of each one.

Expressing Time:
Verbs and Adverbs *Present, Past, and*
Future Time Expressions; Continuous Forms;
Two-Word Verbs and Verbs
with Prepositional Phrases

PASSAGE FOR STUDY

How Different Cultures View Time

All men perceive the distinction between present, past, and future time, although they may have different ways of indicating it in their languages. Yet not all cultures view time in the same way or mark the same time-distinctions in their speech.

In societies based on European culture, people look back on an event in the past. We say, "I enjoyed the concert last night." "Last week I went to Chicago." "I passed my examinations a year ago." In English the verb form and the adverb indicate that these events are past. We say that they are behind us. Similarly we look forward to the future. We say, "I am going to take a trip to Europe next year. I will leave in March." The future, which is indicated in English by an auxiliary verb with the main verb and by an adverb, is before us. For the Quechua Indians of Peru and Bolivia, however, the situation is different. They speak of the future as "behind one-self" and the past as ahead. They argue, "If you can think of the past and the future, which can you see with your mind's eye?" The obvious answer is that we can see the past and not the future, to which the Quechua replies, "Then, if you can see the past, it must be ahead of you, and the future, which you cannot see, is behind you."[1]

Not only is this view of past and future different from that of many cultures with which we may be familiar, but also different languages mark different time distinctions within the present, past, or future, or different relations between periods of time. The speaker of English may say, "I work in the library," and call this present tense even though at the moment of speaking, the true "present time," he is eating lunch with a friend. Confusion exists because what we call present tense does not necessarily refer to the present moment. Action occurring or a situation existing at the actual present is marked with a special form, the "present continuous." This distinction between permanent condition and present occurrence is worth making for the speaker of English, although this distinction is less closely observed in many languages closely related to English.

These differences may suggest that there is more than one valid way of viewing "the same thing" or that there may be differences of opinion as to what "the same thing" really is.

Present Tense

The present tense in English is used for assertions. It is used when one wishes to state what is permanently true, or what is true over a period of time, not merely true for the moment of speaking. It is also used to state opinions or beliefs. Examples of the present tense from the passage you have just read are:

All men *perceive* the distinction between present and past.
Not all cultures *view* time in the same way.

These are statements of fact, or permanent conditions. Other examples of uses of the present tense are:

The State of Hawaii *consists* of seven principal islands. (present fact)
The hiking club *goes* on a picnic every weekend. (repeated action)
This milk *tastes* sour. (opinion)

---

[1] Material on Quechua Indians from Eugene Nida in *Customs and Culture* (New York: Harper & Row, 1954), p. 206.

Note that the present tense adds –s in the third person singular.

Compare:

All men *perceive* . . .
The hiking club *goes* . . .

▶ **Exercise 1**

Study the verb forms used in the selection "Adventure on the Colorado" in the previous lesson. Be able to explain orally or in writing why the present tense is used in these sentences:

1. Many oarsmen *regard* the Colorado as the roughest navigable river in the world.
2. As it *flows* through the 285-mile long Grand Canyon, it *drops* 2,000 feet and *contains* more than 150 rapids.
3. The trip *begins* some miles above the canyon.
4. A motorized barge *makes* the trip in eight or ten days.
5. Suddenly the calmness *vanishes*.
6. The boats often *upset*.
7. In the most dangerous places the guides *advise* the passengers to get out and walk.

▶ **Exercise 2**

Write a paragraph about the importance of one of the following:

water	snow
hurricanes	rivers (or one river)
wild animals	forests (or one forest)
the seasons (or one season)	precious stones

In an opening topic sentence, state what the importance of your subject is, or that the subject has many uses, or take a point of view toward it. Examples of topic sentences are:

Wind

Topic sentence: In this modern scientific age when jet propulsion and atomic energy are important sources of power, it is easy to forget that wind still affects the life of men in many ways.

Summer

Topic sentence: Some people prefer the snows of winter, or the gentle showers of spring, or autumn with its brilliant colors, but summer is my favorite season.

Make four or five statements of fact or opinion in the present tense to support your topic sentence.

Present Continuous

To indicate action that is continuing at the moment of speaking, or to describe a situation that exists at the present moment but which is not a permanent condition, the English language uses *is* or *are* plus the present participle (v + *–ing*). This verb phrase is called the present continuous. The following examples show the forms of the present continuous and the purposes for which it is used:

A. To express action in progress at the moment of speaking:

I speak five languages (permanent condition), but I *am speaking* English now.

B. To describe a situation existing at present:

As I write this, I *am sitting* in front of my fireplace in which a cheerful fire *is roaring*. My wife *is sitting* opposite me. She *is reading* a magazine. The cat *is sleeping* peacefully on the hearth rug. A cold wind *is blowing* outside, but we feel warm and comfortable here by our cozy fire.

Note that present sensations are expressed in the present tense, not the present continuous:

We feel warm.
The food tastes good.

C. To indicate an activity or situation that is continuing over a period of time:

This year I *am studying* biology, English, mathematics, and history at the university. I *am living* in an apartment on Twelfth Street. Here I have fewer interruptions than I had in the dormitory, and I *am making* good progress in my studies. I *am working* harder than I did last year, but I *am enjoying* my work more.

▶ **Exercise 3**

Write four pairs of sentences like those illustrating the first use of the continuous present. Tell what you are doing at the moment or will do sometime today in contrast to the condition that is generally true, or what you generally do at that time of day.

Example
    I like to sleep in the afternoon, but this afternoon I am attending an English class.

Past Tense and Past Continuous

The simple past tense is used to make statements of fact or opinion about conditions in the past.

Examples
    My grandmother's garden contained many varieties of flowers. (The garden no longer exists.) (statement of a fact that was true once but is true no longer)
    The concert last night was not well done. (opinion about a past event)

To indicate action that was continuing at a point of time in the past or to describe a situation or condition in the past, English uses *was* or *were* plus the present participle (v + *–ing*). This is the past continuous form. Note the examples that follow.

A. To report an action that was in process or was continuing at a specific moment in the past or at a time when another event occurred:

    By 1860 the Mississippi Valley *was becoming* settled.
    We *were trying* to get pictures of the parade when the wind blew our camera over.

B. To describe a situation existing in the past:

The scene, as I gazed on it in the late afternoon sunlight, was peaceful and quiet. A few palm trees *were swaying* gently in the breezes. The surf *was lapping* against the shore with a soothing sound. A lone fisherman *was walking* along the beach looking for a place to cast his nets, and a few seagulls *were flying* overhead. There was nothing to indicate that in a very few minutes the hurricane would transform this quiet beach into a place of violence and destruction.

Past tense irregular verb forms are listed in the Appendix, pp. 232–233.

▶ **Exercise 4**

Imagine a scene that is peaceful, boring, exciting, confusing, or that can be described by some other adjective of your choosing. Tell what *is happening* or *was happening* to make you characterize the scene as you have. Model your paragraph on the example of the descriptive use of the present continuous or the past continuous, as just given. Your topic sentence may come at the beginning, as in the example of the past continuous, or at the end, or it may be implied. Make sure all of your details contribute to one impression. Use present continuous or past continuous verb forms.

▶ **Exercise 5**

Complete these sentences to tell what event happened when people were doing each of the following:

1. I was ringing the doorbell when . . .
2. The policeman was just entering the intersection on his motorcycle when . . .
3. The general was just lighting his pipe when . . .
4. The jewel thieves were sneaking away from the party when . . .
5. The surgeon was raising his scalpel to make the incision when . . .

Expressions of Future Time

There is no one special verb form to indicate future time in English. The future is indicated by verb phrases, or sometimes by the present tense and an adverb, as follows:

a. *going to* + VERB

> I am *going to take* a trip next week. (planned or intended action)

b. *will* + VERB

> I *will be* in Washington for a week. (promise, or statement of simple futurity)
> My wife Sarah *will go* with me.

c. present tense + adverbial element indicating time

> Our plane *leaves at eight o'clock.* (usually used for schedules)

Shall is sometimes used with *I* or *we* in expressions of future time.

> I *shall be* in Washington for a week. *Will* you *be* there then?

In questions *will* expresses futurity.

> *Will* I *see* you when I get there?

Shall expresses advisability.

> *Shall* I *pack* my raincoat for the Washington trip?

▶ **Exercise 6**

Assume you have a friend who has visited a place where you would like to go. Write two paragraphs of a letter to him (or her). Begin the first paragraph:

> (Next week/next summer) I'm going to take a trip to (place).

Add a few sentences telling what you intend to do while you are there and what you will probably see or visit.

In the second paragraph state that because your friend has been there you would like some advice from him. Develop this paragraph with four or five questions asking for information, help, or advice. Have at least one question of each type.

Examples
Will I need my raincoat? (request for information)
Will you send me the addresses of your friends who live there? (request for help)
Shall I call your friends when I get there? (request for advice)

Two-Word Verbs

A number of verbs are regularly followed by adverbs which modify or change their meaning. These are called two-word verbs. When the object of such a verb is a noun, the adverb may stand next to the verb or at the end of the sentence.

He *brought back* the book.
He *brought* the book *back*.

When the object is a pronoun, the adverb part of the two-word verb stands at the end.

He *brought* it *back*.

Common adverb particles in the two-word verb pattern are *back, up, out, down, over, away.*

▶ **Exercise 7**

Complete a reply to each of the following comments or questions. Use the indicated two-word verb with a pronoun object. The following example uses the two-word verb *find out:*

Comment: I'd like to know who won the Indianapolis 500 (an automobile race).
Reply: We can *find that out* when we listen to the news tonight.

1. *fill out*

   Comment: I'm having trouble with this questionnaire.
   Reply: Let me help you _____.

2. *call up* (telephone)

   Comment: I called up my friend John last night to get the
   English assignment, but he wasn't home.
   Reply: Why didn't you _____?

3. *use up* (finish the supply of)

   Comment: What happened to all the carbon paper? I can't
   find any.
   Reply: I _____.

4. *give away* (get rid of)

   Comment: I can't find my old slippers anywhere. Have you
   seen them?
   Reply: Oh, I'm sorry, George. They were so old that I
   _____.

5. *help out* (aid)

   Comment: Many foreign students have problems in writing
   term papers. Maybe you can show them what to do.
   Reply: I'll be glad to _____.

6. *finish up* (complete)

   Comment: When do you expect to finish up the project you
   are working on?
   Reply: I think I can _____ tomorrow.

7. *try out* (test)

   Comment: I'd like to try out the new motorbike that I bought
   yesterday.
   Reply: Maybe you can _____ this evening.

8. *put on* (garment, clothing)

   Comment: I think it's cold outside. You'd better put on your
   sweater.
   Reply: If it's cold I'll _____ when I get outside.

Verbs and Adjectives
with Prepositional Phrases

Some verbs and adjectives are followed by certain prepositions in idiomatic expressions.

Examples
We must *decide on* a plan of action.
Don't be *angry about* the decision.

A list of verb-preposition and adjective-preposition combinations is found in the Appendix, pp. 245–246.

▶ **Exercise 8**

Write a paragraph of a few sentences about someone you know. Begin with a sentence using an adjective plus a prepositional phrase that characterizes the person in some way.

Example
(Name of person) is very *different from me.*

Tell some of the following things about him, using these adjectives or verbs with prepositions, or others from the list in the Appendix, pp. 245–246.

What he *is interested in*   What he *is fond of*
What he *is proud of*   What he *is content with*
What he *is accustomed to*   What he *has respect for*
What he *is tired of*   What he *is annoyed by*

▶ **Exercise 9**

Answer these questions orally or in writing about the structure of the essay "How Different Cultures View Time."

1. The first sentence serves as an introduction to the second, in that the second sentence qualifies it. What word in the second sentence shows the qualification or limitation?
2. The thesis sentence (second sentence of the first paragraph) indicates that two things will be discussed in the following paragraphs. What are they?

3. Which of the two topics indicated in the thesis sentence is discussed in the second paragraph? Which is discussed in the third?
4. What is the relation of the last paragraph to the first?

Composition

There is an old saying that no man can step in the same river twice. One might change the saying to read: "The same man never steps in a river twice." This would be one way of saying that a person is changed by what happens to him, by what he reads, by the people he comes in contact with—by the mere fact of becoming older.

Use the following statement as the thesis sentence of a short composition.

The process of maturing involves many changes in a person's life.

Discuss how this applies to yourself. You will probably mention beliefs you once held but no longer accept, some activities you engaged in at one time but no longer enjoy, some personal relationships that existed for you then but no longer exist, or some personal habits (eating, grooming, caring for your belongings, getting work done, engaging in recreational activities) you have abandoned, or interests you at one time had but no longer have. Conclude with a statement about what may be the situation in the future with regard to these activities, habits, or beliefs.

Expressing Relationships in Time *Perfect Verb Forms; Positions of Adverbs*

Undersea Museums[1]

Throughout the United States there are many campgrounds that the Department of the Interior of the federal government has established at places of historic or scenic interest. Those at Yellowstone Park, the Grand Canyon, or the battlefield at Gettysburg, Pennsylvania are examples. These camping places have become more and more crowded during the last few years as an increasing number of families take their vacations by car or camper. Until recently, however, no one had thought of using the resources of the underwater areas off the coasts as recreation areas. Now since scuba[2] diving has become so popular, four undersea areas have been set aside as retreats for swimmers and divers who want to get away from the crowds found in most vacation areas.

The explorations of the French oceanographer Jacques Costeau and his son Philippe brought to world attention the ships and planes that were wrecked off Truk Island in Micronesia in World War II. In 1972 the U.S. government declared this area a national monument. Since then, many adventurous scuba divers have been

---

[1] Facts taken from Thomas Ciafardoni, "Underwater Parks: Keep 'Em Coming" *True,* vol. 54, no. 430 (March 1973), 30.

[2] *Scuba* stands for "*self-contained underwater breathing apparatus.*"

able to explore the hulks of some seventy sunken ships in a park that is both eerie and fascinating. More recently, the U.S. government has established Buck Island Reef National Monument just off St. Croix in the Virgin Islands, and has set up underwater markers to identify the coral. The government has even put up picture markers giving the names and habits of the fish.

The first subsurface park in the continental United States was established at Key Largo, Florida. It covers some seventy-five square miles, and gives the diver his only chance to see living coral in North American waters. To date more than three million people have enjoyed the many types of coral on the reef and the varieties of fish that go swimming by.

Another undersea museum has recently been set aside at Big Sur, California. It adjoins a park area along the shore.

Since the advent of scuba in 1943, adventurers under the sea have shown that they can venture almost anywhere. Perhaps in the future the sea will have become nearly the only place where man can retire to find the solitude he once found in the vast empty areas of the land.

Present Perfect

As we have noted in Lesson 3, English distinguishes continuing action from permanent condition, and indicates the difference between present, past, and future time. In this lesson we see that it also indicates relationships between present and past time or present and future time or among all three time periods. The relationship between past time and the present moment is shown by the use of *has* (*have*) plus the past participle (v–*ed, –en*). This form is called the present perfect. It is used throughout the passage "Undersea Museums" to indicate what has been accomplished up to the present moment (the moment of writing). This time relationship is not expressed in the same way in other languages, but it is widely used in English. Thus it needs careful study.

The uses of the present perfect may be summarized as follows, with examples contrasting its use with that of the past tense.

1. To express a condition that has existed in the past up to the present moment, and is still true at present:

I was in England for one year. (The speaker is no longer there.)

I *have been* in England for one year. (The speaker is still in England.)

2. To express action which has (or has not) occurred in the past and which may (or may not) occur again in the future:

An old man says, "I was in Paris once." (He does not expect to go again.)

A young man says. "I *have been* to Paris once." (He may go again.)

3. To express recency of action or condition:

I finished my assignment. (The finishing took place at some time in the past. It is now past history.)

I *have just finished* my assignment. (The speaker expresses the recency of the completion of the action. *Just, just recently,* and other adverbs with similar meanings are often used when this meaning is expressed.)

4. To indicate that an act was complete before the moment of speaking:

Are you going to get the car repaired today? I *have already done* it.

Can you get the report done by tomorrow? I *have already finished* it. (The speaker speaks of an act in reference to the moment of speaking. The adverb *already* is used.)

▶ **Exercise 1**

Explain orally why you think the present perfect was used in the following sentences adapted from "Undersea Museums." You may want to refer to the preceding list of uses of the present perfect.

1. The Department of the Interior *has established* campgrounds at places of historic or scenic interest.
2. These camping places *have become* more and more crowded.
3. Since scuba diving *has become* so popular, four undersea areas *have been set aside.*

4. Since then, many adventurous scuba divers *have been able* to explore the hulks of some seventy sunken ships.
5. The government *has set up* underwater markers to identify the coral.
6. To date more than three million people *have enjoyed* the many types of coral.
7. Perhaps in the future the sea *will have become* nearly the only place where man can retire to find the solitude he once found in the vast empty areas of the land.

▶ **Exercise 2**

Study the verb forms in the following two passages:

1. Last month I *went* to Washington. I *visited* the White House. I *saw* the Capitol, and *watched* the proceedings of the Senate from the visitors' gallery. The Smithsonian Institution *interested* me greatly. It *helped* me understand the development of the country.

2. Now I can tell my friends that I *have been* to Washington, I *have visited* the White House, I *have* seen the Capitol, and *have watched* the proceedings of the Senate. During my visit the Smithsonian Institution *interested* me greatly. It *helped* me understand the development of the country.

Answer the following questions:

1. From what point of time is the action being discussed in each passage?
2. What words at the beginning of each passage indicate the point of time?
3. Why are forms with *have* + v–*ed*, –*en* (present perfect) used in the second passage but not in the first?
4. Why are the verbs in the last two sentences in the second passage in the simple past tense?

▶ **Exercise 3**

Assume that you are interviewing one of your classmates for a job. Decide what the job is. Then list six questions that you, as a prospective employer, might ask in order to find out whether he is capable of handling the job. Choose some line of work you know well.

Example
  A rice farmer in Arkansas might ask a man applying for a job on his farm:

  1. Have you ever surveyed for levees?
  2. Have you ever run a tractor?
  3. Have you had any experience with electric pumps?
  4. Have you ever run a combine?

Continuous Present Perfect

Just as English uses a continuous form of the present and past tenses, there are also continuous forms of the perfect tenses. Continuous perfect verb phrases indicate both duration and recency.

Compare:

  John *has read* a great many novels. (He has read them sometime before the moment of speaking.)
  John *has been reading* a great many novels. (He has been reading them over a period of time just before and up to the moment of speaking.)
  I *have lived* here for a year. (I still live here.)
  I *have been living* here for a year. (I still live here, but the duration of the condition is emphasized.)

▶ **Exercise 4**

Write a paragraph about the interests and activities of the most fascinating person you know. Use as your topic sentence:

(Name of person) is a person of many interests.

Use perfect constructions with *has* (in both the simple and the continuous form) when appropriate, to tell some of the things that the person you are writing about *has done* or *has been doing* recently.

John Jones is a person of many interests. He *has studied* photography, chemistry, and art, and *has displayed* his photographs in a number of exhibitions. Because he knows chemistry, he develops his pictures himself, and *has perfected* a new process to produce them quickly.

Past Perfect

The past perfect (*had* + v–*ed*, –*en*) is used when the writer or speaker wants to refer to an event that happened before another event in the past, or to a condition that continued up to a time in the past.

Examples
Mr. Howard *sank* down exhausted. He *had shaken* hands with at least a thousand people during the political rally.
The bus finally *started*. The luggage *had delayed* the departure.

▶ **Exercise 5**

Write four pairs of sentences. In the second sentence of each pair, refer to action that was completed prior to the action referred to in the first sentence. The second sentence will contain a verb in the past perfect with *had*.

Example
The postman *came* back to the office with more mail.
He *had* already *delivered* two packages earlier in the day.

▶ **Exercise 6**

Here is the beginning of a little narrative about an absent-minded friend. Finish the narrative by telling of other absent-minded mistakes he made that day. Use *had* + v–*ed*, –*en* as often as possible.

My Absent-Minded Friend

John, my friend who is working on his Ph.D. degree in physics, is a likable fellow, but he is quite absent-minded. He causes himself a great deal of trouble because he does not keep his mind on the practical matters of living. The other day he went to buy a suit and got halfway downtown before he realized that he had left his billfold at home. He returned to his room to get it, and then went downtown again. When he opened the billfold to pay for the suit, he found it empty. Then he remembered that he had spent all his money the day before, buying some books that he wanted for his library. So he needed to write a check to pay for the suit. When he reached into his pocket to get his checkbook, he could not find it, and then he remembered that he had . . .

▶ **Exercise 7**

A common use of *had* + v–*ed, –en* is in reported speech.

Examples
Quoted: John said, "I *took* the examination this morning."
Reported: John said that he *had taken* the examination this morning.
Quoted: John asked, *"Did* I *pass?"*
Reported: John asked whether (if) he *had passed.*

Rewrite the following conversation to report what the two speakers said.

PROFESSOR: I have just read the examination papers.

JOHN: Did I pass?

PROFESSOR: You passed, but you did not do as well as I had hoped.

JOHN: I studied until three o'clock in the morning.

PROFESSOR: That's probably why you didn't do well. You didn't have enough sleep.

JOHN: But if I don't study, I don't know the material, and I can't study when I am sleeping.

PROFESSOR: If you had studied every day, you wouldn't have to study so much at the last minute.

Continuous Past Perfect

The continuous form of the past perfect (I *had been studying,* he *had been sleeping,* they *had been talking*) places emphasis on the continuing of an act or a condition up to a specific time in the past. This form of the verb is not common, but it is used occasionally.

Compare:

He *had lived* there a year when he decided to move to the suburbs.

He *had been living* there a year when he decided to move to the suburbs. (The emphasis is on the continuing of the condition.)

▶ **Exercise 8**

A. Explain why the continuous form with *had been* is appropriate in each of these sentences:

1. Bill *had been taking* violin lessons for ten years before he gave his first concert.
2. We *had been watching* television shows for years before we learned how television really works.
3. The members of the group *had been studying* art for a long time by themselves before they decided to form a club to study it formally.

B. Write four sentences like the previous ones. Contrast the use of the past perfect continuous with the past tense.

Adverbs and Adverbial Phrases

Adverbs and phrases used as adverbs may be used with a verb to show location. (See Sentence Pattern 1 and Sentence Pattern 6 in Lesson 1.) They are also a means of indicating time (as in Lesson 3):

The plane leaves *at six o'clock.*

Adverbs and adverbials also show manner.

Examples
My secretary does her job *well.*
The children came *quickly.*
They came *in a hurry.*

Phrases with *to* and a verb, or with *in order to,* show purpose.

Examples
I went to the store *to buy a loaf of bread.*
We left early *in order to be there when the play started.*

The adverb is the most movable element in the sentence. The usual position is at the end of the sentence, but the adverb may also be found at the beginning of the sentence, or before the verb. If the sentence is long, one adverbial element usually stands at the beginning, particularly if one is a phrase or clause of time or place.

Examples
In the summertime when the days are long, I *often* get up *early* and take a long walk *before breakfast. Whenever I go on these walks,* I can *usually* see the mountains *clearly.*

Note that except in the case of two-word verbs (Lesson 3), the one place where the adverb is almost never placed in an English sentence is between the verb and object or complement—a common position for the adverb in many other languages. For example, it is incorrect in English to say, "You will see on your right tall buildings."

Following is a summary of the placement of adverbs.

At the end of the sentence

This is the most common position of adverbs.

Examples adapted from "Undersea Museums":
These camping places have become more and more crowded *during the last few years.*
The fish go swimming *by.*
Another undersea museum has recently been set aside *at Big Sur, California.*

At the beginning of the sentence

Any adverbial of time, place, manner, or purpose may stand at the beginning of the sentence. In this position it modifies the sentence.

Examples

In 1972 the U.S. government declared this area a national monument. (time)

Throughout the United States there are many campgrounds that the Department of the Interior has established. (place)

By swimming you can reach these underwater museums. (manner)

To get to these museums, you must use scuba-diving equipment. (purpose)

In a s–v sentence pattern, adverbials of place generally stand at the end of the sentence: s–v–ADV. However, this sentence pattern may be inverted as ADV–v–s to place the emphasis on the subject.

Examples

A dark shadow lay *on the floor.*   s–v–ADV

On the floor lay a dark shadow.   ADV–v–s **(The emphasis is on the dark shadow.)**

Before the verb

Two kinds of adverbs are placed before the verb:

1. Common single-word adverbs of time such as *then, now, soon, always, often, seldom, sometimes, usually, just, almost, ever,* and *never.* Most of these indicate indefinite time. *Now, then,* and *soon* commonly appear at the end of the sentence also.

When a verb is preceded by an auxiliary these adverbs generally stand before the main verb after the auxiliary.

Examples

People can *now* visit underwater museums.

I have *never* visited an underwater museum.

Note that with the perfect forms of the verb, the adverb goes before the participle. With the perfect continuous forms, the adverb follows *have.*

The professor has *sometimes* been giving us short tests.

2. Most adverbs of manner end in *-ly*. These adverbs may stand at the beginning or the end of the sentence or (most commonly) before the verb.

Examples
   Hastily the thief destroyed the evidence.
   The thief destroyed the evidence *hastily*.
   The thief *hastily* destroyed the evidence.

▶ **Exercise 9**

In the following passages underline the modifiers of verbs. Read the passages aloud and be prepared to explain why the author placed the modifiers where he did. For each sentence that you read aloud, consider whether the adverbial element could be placed in another position. Would the sentence be as effective?

1. After careful discussion the Senate last week passed the education bill by an overwhelming majority.
2. I didn't see him at all yesterday because I wasn't here then.
3. We actually got there early by driving continuously from eight A.M. until noon.
4. "In *Fishing for Fun* . . . Herbert Hoover has pieced together with a needle of humor his meditations on his favorite sport. He got his baptism of worm fishing in the creeks of Iowa, but at the age of ten he was transported to Oregon, where access to the mountain streams and the gift of three artificial flies opened a new vista."[3]
5. As we approached, the house appeared deserted. The moonlight lay cold and still around us. Not a sound was to be heard but our own footsteps, which echoed hollowly on the cobblestones. We paused. A noise—a harsh, rasping noise—came to our ears in pulsing rhythm. We froze a moment, unable to move, and stifled an impulse to run madly from the place. Then, at the realization that it was our own heavy breathing that we heard, relief flooded us. Gathering our courage, we strode forward

---

[3] Edward Weeks, "The Paripatetic Reporter," *Atlantic*, 212 (October 1963), 146.

boldly, telling ourselves that there was no cause for alarm. We had only to enter the house, turn on the lights, and we would find, as reason would have us believe, that nobody was there. The door was now but a few feet before us. We approached. Our hands were nearly on the knob. Then, just as we were about to push it open, before our incredulous eyes the door began to move slowly inward. And then, and then, around the edge of the door there appeared. . . . I dare not say what. This time we did run—madly, screaming, never pausing to look back.

PASSAGE FOR STUDY

Weathermaking[4]

(1) Ever since the dawn—no doubt the cloudy dawn—of time, man has been trying to change the weather. (2) For a long while he relied on magic and prayer; later he switched to what he can loosely call science. . . .

(3) Until quite recently, all such efforts failed. (4) Only within the last fifteen years—since a young scientist hit upon the technique called cloud-seeding—have we made any real progress. (5) And even the first experiments with that method, after raising excited hopes, proved disappointing.

(6) Cloud-seeding . . . has touched off one of the most baffling controversies in meterological history. (7) It has been blamed for, or credited with, practically all kinds of weather. (8) Some scientists claim seeding can produce floods or hail. (9) Others insist it creates droughts and dissipates clouds. (10) Still others staunchly maintain it has no effect at all. (11) The battle is far from over, but at least one clear conclusion is beginning to emerge; man *can* change the weather, and he is getting better at it.

▸ **Exercise 10**

The passage "Weathermaking" illustrates many of the grammatical points you have been studying in this lesson. It also shows that effective communication is related to how you handle sentences. Answer the following questions based on the passage:

[4] William C. Vergara, "Weathermaking, a Dream That May Come True," *Harper's Magazine,* January 1962, 56.

1. What is the interrupting element in sentence 1? What sentence element does it repeat? This inserted element arouses the reader's curiosity by hinting at the central idea without revealing it. What word in this interrupting element gives an idea of what the central idea is to be?

2. In paragraph 2 the writer might have said, "In the last fifteen years men have had questionable success in producing rain by cloud-seeding." However, instead of doing this he calls attention to his ideas by unexpected changes in the sentence patterns. What is the interrupting element in sentence 4? In sentence 5?

3. Why does the author make "or credited with" stand out in sentence 7, when in sentence 8, 9, and 10 he shows that people consider cloud-seeding a failure? Would a reader want to read about a scientific experiment that has failed? In what sense has cloud-seeding not failed?

4. Reread sentences 1, 4, 5, and 7, omitting the interrupting elements. Is the dramatic effect of each sentence and of the paragraph as a whole the same?

   Warning: Make sparing use of this method of making ideas dramatic. If an orchestra plays forte constantly, it cannot produce a fortissimo climax. You cannot be dramatic all the time. Do not use interrupting elements just to make clear what you should have stated clearly in the first place.

5. Why is a perfect or continuous form of the verb used in sentences 1, 5, and 6? Why is the past tense used in sentences 2 and 3? Why is a continuous form of the verb used in two sentence patterns in sentence 11?

▶ **Exercise 11**

Write three sentences expressing the type of action suggested in each of the following.

1. Action you completed at some time in the past:

   Yesterday I *went* downtown.

2. Action you have repeated *since* a certain time in the past:

   I *have gone* downtown three times since ten o'clock.

3. Something you have been doing continuously for a period of time:

I *have been going* there once a day for the last three months.
I *have been standing* on this corner since ten o'clock.

▶ **Exercise 12**

Part of the effectiveness of the paragraph on weathermaking depends upon the pattern of the organization. Note the different markers used to indicate progression in time and in numbers.

Time: in sentence 1, *ever since*
          in sentence 2, *for a long while* and *later*
          in sentence 3, *until quite recently*
          in sentence 4, *only within the last fifteen years*
Number: in sentence 8, *some scientists*
          in sentence 9, *others*
          in sentence 10, *still others*

Write short paragraphs on subjects of your own choosing in which you can make use of (1) a series of time markers and (2) a series of number markers.

Composition

Note that "Weathermaking" is organized chronologically (in the order of time). The passage tells what man *has been doing in the past* to change the weather, and ends with the comment that *at present he is getting better at it.*

Write a composition of about two paragraphs on A, B, or C, which follow. Your organizational pattern in each case should be chronological.

A. What *has* some person or some group of people *done* or *been doing* to contribute to the culture of your country? Use as your topic sentence:

(Person or group) has done a great deal (or, a great many things) to contribute to the culture of (or accomplish a particular goal in) my country.

The example in Exercise 4 in this lesson may give you some suggestions.

B. What progress has been made toward accomplishing some practical goal in your country: for example, to improve education, to establish a better system of government, to improve relations with other countries, and so on? Use as your topic sentence:

For _____ years we have been trying to develop better __ in (country).

As in the passage "Weathermaking," tell what someone *did* at some time in the past, what *was being done* before changes were made, and what *is being done* now.

C. How has some event affected you? How has it changed your beliefs or your way of living? Use as your topic sentence:

(Event) has had a great effect on me (or has changed my way of thinking).

Tell what you *believed in* or *did* before the event; then tell what you *have done* or *have accomplished* or *have believed* since the event occurred, and what you *have been doing* recently.

Describing with Adjectivals and Passive Forms
Adjectives and Phrases as Modifiers of Nouns, Qualifiers of Adjectives; Uses of the Passive Voice

Adjectivals

PASSAGE FOR STUDY

The Old and the New[1]

In the oases [of the Arab world], large and small, Arab men and women weave the distinctive fabric of their life. New factories are breaking the monopoly of pyramids; new habits clash with old; yet within it all there is a fusion and a unity.

The fabric is visible in multitudinous details. A bearded old man, white turban wound tightly around his red fez, punctures the cold hours before dawn with his age-old cry: "Prayer is better than sleep!" A jet streaks through the pale sky as donkeys patter through village lanes. In government offices and in the bazaars, there is the rattle of spoons in glasses of mint tea. There is the hum of gossip as bolts of vivid cloth are unrolled before dark-eyed women. In coffee shops, the radio . . . blares the news of the day. In curbside stalls boys fan charcoal as meat is grilled. A scent of spice makes

---

[1] Desmond Stewart and the editors of *Life,* "The Arab World" (copyright Time Incorporated, 1962), p. 10. Used by permission.

an ordinary street mysterious, and when the day ends, the night, identified in Arab poetry with the lover, brings magic under the sapphire stars. From the desert, beyond the minarets and palm trees, come the howls of jackals.

▶ **Exercise 1**

Adjectives and other modifiers of nouns give details to make ideas vivid. Answer the following questions on the passage "The Old and the New."

1. What assertion do the details in this paragraph support?
2. To what senses does this description appeal? List some visual details that are static, and some that give a sense of movement.
3. Underline all of the descriptive words that precede nouns. These are largely single-word adjectives. Note the form of these words. (The adjective in English does *not* change form to agree with the noun.)
4. Which of these adjectives do you consider particularly effective?
5. Underline the modifiers that follow the noun. (Examples are "oases, *large* and *small*," "the monopoly *of pyramids*," etc.) Are these prepositional phrases, participles, or other types of structure? Note that they consist of more than one word.
6. What class of words other than adjectives makes you able to picture life in the Arab world? (Examples: "donkeys *patter*," "Arab men and women *weave* the distinctive fabric of their life") List other particularly effective examples.
7. Note some of the ways in which variety is obtained: by different types of sentence patterns, by varied types and varied placement of modifiers of nouns. Find examples of each of these devices.

Forms and Qualifiers of Adjectives

Adjectives in English may change form only to show degree.

Examples

| long | longer | longest |
| good | better | best[a] |

[a] This is one of the few irregular adjectives.

Adjectives of more than one syllable generally do not change form to show degree, but they are qualified or intensified, often by *more* or *most*.

Example
expensive   more expensive   most expensive

Other common qualifiers of adjectives follow, arranged roughly so that those indicating a lesser degree of qualification are at the left and those indicating a greater degree of qualification are at the right:

a bit	less	awfully	so
a little	more	indeed	least
just	enough	pretty	most
more or less		quite	too
rather		really	very
somewhat			

Enough is generally placed after the adjective, unless the comparative form of the adjective is being used.

Example
It is *good enough* to be worth the money.
(But: If it is *enough cheaper,* I'll buy it.)

Position of Adjectives

Adjectives generally precede the noun. A pair of adjectives or an adjectival phrase may come after the noun for special emphasis. Such an adjectival is generally separated from the rest of the sentence by commas.

Example
In the oases [of the Arab world], *large and small,* . . .

No final rule for the order in a series of adjectives can be set forth. The order depends in part on the relationship of the ideas expressed by the modifiers of the noun. Adjectives expressing nationality, however, generally come last in a series of descriptive words.

Examples
  expensive little French hat
  good German cooking

► **Exercise 2**

Write a paragraph describing the highlights of the fabric of life in your culture, or of some place you have visited and observed. Model your description on the passage "The Old and the New." Include details that appeal to the senses—sound, sight, touch, smell, taste—as the author of the description of life in the Arab world has done. Note the topic sentence of that passage: "Within it all there is a fusion and a unity." In your description include a sentence that characterizes what you are describing.

PASSAGE FOR STUDY

The Qualities of a Leader

The man whom I would choose to lead my country should be a man of more than ordinary vision and judgment. He should be a man capable of guiding the nation wisely and firmly through difficult times, undaunted by the responsibilities of his position. He should be a man adept in dealing with people of diverse backgrounds, personalities, and interests, a man calm in difficult situations. He should have insight enough to anticipate a crisis and meet it with strength and determination, and the courage to act as his beliefs and conscience tell him. He should be a man unwilling to compromise his principles for personal gain. His office calls for a leader educated not only through reading but also through experience. Such men are described in John F. Kennedy's book *Profiles in Courage.*

► **Exercise 3**

Answer the following questions about the paragraph you have just read.

1. What is the central idea of the paragraph?
2. What is the function of the last sentence?
3. List six different modifiers that follow the noun they modify.

Identify the modifier as a prepositional phrase, adjective and qualifier, or participle. (Note "a leader *educated through experience*.")

▶ **Exercise 4**

Write a paragraph similar to "The Qualities of a Leader" telling what kind of person you would want to do one of the following:

1. direct an entertainment program
2. become your husband or wife
3. teach your children
4. become your friend

Use structures of modification following the noun. You may want to include some of the following:

1. a person with experience in ⸺⸺⸺
2. a person used to meeting unusual circumstances
3. a woman of intelligence and sound judgment

End your paragraph by suggesting a possible person or type of person to fill the position or perform the activity.

Passive Verb Forms

PASSAGE FOR STUDY

The Throne Room[2]

(1) So that he might enjoy the brilliant colours of his flower-beds in winter-time, the king had them copied into a vast carpet some thirty-five yards square. (2) This carpet, called "Chosroes' Spring-

---

[2] Ernst Diez, *In the Ancient Worlds of Asia,* trans. by W. C. Darwell from the French version by Louis Mezeray (New York: Putnam's, 1961), p. 92. © Macdonald and Co. (Publishers) Ltd., 1961.

time," was laid in the throne-room in the winter for use by the king and his court at festivals.

(3) It was the largest carpet ever made and was woven in threads of silk, gold and silver and set with precious stones. (4) The design represented a pleasure-garden with streams, paths, trees and flowers. (5) The yellowish soil was made of gold with the banks of the streams in a darker colour; the water was represented by threads of silver and the pebbles at the bottom and the fish were woven in their natural colours. (6) The gravel of the paths was worked in small stones the size of pearls; (7) the stalks of the plants and the branches were in silver and gold, all the leaves were made of silk and the fruits were many-coloured precious stones.

(8) The eighth wonder of the world had a modest posterity which continued down to the "garden carpets" of the eighteenth century. (9) According to the Arab and Persian historians of the time, the walls of the throne room, of which the bare bricks are still standing, were once covered with mosaics. (10) These portrayed, amongst other things, a scene from the siege of Antioch and the fighting round the town. (11) Here Chrosroes, in a green tunic on a red-roan horse, is reviewing his troops. (12) The lower part of the walls was hung with carpets and the back of the room, containing the throne, was divided off by a huge brocade curtain.

The Passive Voice

The selection "The Throne Room," like the others in this lesson, is descriptive. It tells of a palace in an ancient capital in Asia Minor. Part of the throne room is still standing today, and the author of the book goes into some detail about the furnishings of that room as it was in the days of its glory. The description in this selection is presented largely through the use of the passive voice, that is, *be* and the past participle (v–*ed*, –*en*).

Examples

The carpet *was woven* in threads of silk, gold and silver.

The yellowish soil *was made* of gold.

The water *was represented* by threads of silver and the pebbles at the bottom and the fish *were woven* in their natural colours.

The passive is also used to state the existence of a condition.

Example
The carpet . . . *was laid* in the throne room.

Generally, when we use the passive voice, we do not know or do not care who performed the act. The focus is on the result of an act, not its performance. For example, we do not know who wove the rug or laid it in the throne room.

While every subject-verb-object pattern sentence may theoretically be put into the passive, relatively few sentences are effective this way.

Compare:

The secretaries are typing the letters. (active)
The letters are being typed by the secretaries. (passive)

The active form of this sentence is more forceful and direct.

▶ **Exercise 5**

In the passage "The Throne Room" find examples of the following:

1. Three other examples of the passive used descriptively (not just to state a condition)
2. Three other descriptive structures

▶ **Exercise 6**

In "The Throne Room" you will find examples of the present continuous form of the verb to show action in progress, as well as the passive to describe or show the results of the completed action.

Compare:

Chosroes . . . *is reviewing* his troops. (action)
The walls *were* once *covered* with mosaics. (result of action)

A. Write a paragraph of a few sentences describing a place where activity is in progress at the moment.

Suggestions:

The street where you live

The marketplace or public park in your town

The room in which you are sitting.

Use present continuous verb forms.

Example

As I look out the window I see a great deal of activity. My neighbor *is building* an addition to his house. He *keeps bringing in* pieces of lumber. At this moment, his helper *is going by* with a wheelbarrow full of sand for concrete. They *are making* a lot of noise when I want to sleep.

B. Describe the same scene, focusing on completed action or description of the scene.

Example

As I *look* out of the window on the street where I *live*, I *can see* my neighbor's house. It *is built* of wood and *is painted* white with green shutters. Rose bushes *are planted* by the side of it. They *are blooming now.* (condition)

PASSAGE FOR STUDY

Orientation Program

A program of orientation has been planned for the new student. Before a boy arrives in the fall he is told what is expected of him. He is sent a booklet of information in which the rules and regulations of the school, the class procedures, and the grading and examination system are set forth. He is assigned a room in the dormitory and is given the name of the boy who will be his roommate. To help him further in adjusting to the new way of life he will be living, the school assigns an upperclassman to be his friend and mentor when he arrives on the campus. On his arrival he will be met by this upperclassman and will be taken on a tour of the campus. While he is being shown the library, gymnasium, and the lecture rooms, his mentor will answer questions that he may have concerning the school and its program.

▶ **Exercise 7**

In the passage about the rug in the throne room, the passive voice was appropriately used because the author did not *know* who made the rug. The paragraph about the orientation program might well appear in a school brochure showing how carefully the school has planned to make a student's first few days at the school easier. The passive is appropriate here because it does not matter to the incoming student just who has done these things for him.

Make a list of passive verb forms that you find in "Orientation Program" and indicate whether they represent present, past, or future time.

▶ **Exercise 8**

The passage about the orientation program was written for a student at a preparatory school. Write a similar passage to be sent to foreign students about the orientation program at the university you are now attending. Use the passive voice.

Composition

The organizational pattern in a descriptive passage is often spatial. The writer describes what he sees or hears or feels as he moves across the scene. Note the order in "The Throne Room."

Write a description of a scene that you have witnessed recently or a place that you have visited. Your instructor may ask you to visit some particular place such as a museum or park for the purposes of this assignment, and to describe what you see there.

Suggestions:

A picture or statue in a local art gallery
An exhibit in a local museum
A public building
A costume that someone wore on a special occasion

Use details to make your description vivid. Include as many of the following kinds of information as possible: (1) what the item you are describing is made *of*, (2) what it is decorated *with*, (3) whom it was made *by*, (4) what colors it is painted *in* (5) what it is used *for*, (6) whom it is used *by*, and so forth. Note the use of prepositions in the passage "The Throne Room" and be careful to select appropriate prepositions in the description that you write. Underline the verbs in the passive voice.

Describing with Relative Clauses and Verbals *Clauses and Reductions of Clauses as Modifiers of Nouns*

PASSAGE FOR STUDY

An Unusual Bequest

The Smithsonian Institution in Washington, D.C. is the largest museum in the world. Its seven buildings and the many acres of land where its outdoor exhibits are located encompass a collection valued at more than a billion dollars. The Smithsonian is an unusual institution, not only in the extent of its collections and the activities it carries on, but also in the manner of its founding.

The countless numbers and variety of items in the Smithsonian have won for it the title "the nation's attic." In it is a vast collection, of which only half a million items—less than one percent of the total—are on display. Many of the displays reflect the growth and development of the republic. The transportation exhibit includes a warship dating from the time of the American Revolution as well as the first spaceship to go to the moon. One locomotive engine in the collection is so large that the building had to be constructed around it. In the display of objects associated with presidents one may see the uniform worn by President Eisenhower when he was a general in the United States Army, a sword belonging to George Washington, shoes made for Thomas Jefferson by one of his slaves, and Herbert Hoover's fishing pole. There are also exhibits representing all fields of science. The National Gallery of Art, containing priceless paintings from all over the world, is part of the Smithsonian.

Most of the eighteen million persons who visit the Smithsonian every year are unaware of the fact that the collection is a basis for research for some three hundred scientists on the permanent staff. Their activities range from the first scientific study of the American Indian to investigations of solar radiation and improvements in home building. The results of their work are reported in the Smithsonian's many publications.

The origin of the Institution is perhaps more unusual than the extent of its collection and the range of its activities. Its founder was James Smithson, an Englishman, who bequeathed his fortune to a country which he had never visited. An illegitimate son of the Duke of Northumberland, he was denied a title and opportunities in England that he felt he should have. Impressed by the work of the British Royal Institution, an organization devoted to making knowledge, especially in the field of science, available to the people, he stated in his will that on his death his fortune should be used "to found at Washington under the name of the Smithsonian Institution an establishment for the increase and diffusion of knowledge among men." Although the fiery U.S. Senator John C. Calhoun declared that "It is beneath the dignity of the United States to accept presents of this kind," Congress grudgingly accepted the gift. In 1838, nine years after Smithson's death, the clipper ship *Mediator* sailed into New York harbor bringing 105 bags of gold sovereigns from his estate. The coins were sent to Philadelphia, where they were melted down and cast into American coins valued at $508,318.46, a not inconsiderable fortune at that time. Congress then set about deciding how to use this amount for the purpose which Smithson had intended. They appointed as the first secretary of the Institution Joseph Henry, the scientist who had worked on the electromagnet. Thus the work of this unusual institution to increase and diffuse knowledge was begun.

Relative Clauses as Modifiers

The selection "An Unusual Bequest" illustrates types of modifiers of nouns in addition to those reviewed in Lesson 5. Note the uses of relative clauses to describe and explain.

the eighteen million persons *who visit the Smithsonian every year* (relative clause—relative pronoun *who* as subject)

country *which he had never visited* (relative clause—relative pronoun *which* as object)

a vast collection, *of which only half a million items . . .* are on display (relative clause—relative pronoun *which* as object of preposition *of*)

acres of land *where its outdoor exhibits are located* (relative clause—*where* as substitute for prepositional phrase *on which*)

Clauses with *that* are also used to give further information about or to complement a noun:

the fact *that* the collection is a basis for research (*That* is used as a subordinating word. It does not substitute for a sentence element.)

Note that relative pronouns are often omitted when they are objects of verbs:

The activities (that) *it carries on.*

▶ **Exercise 1**

Relative clauses may be thought of as resulting from the combination of two sentences containing an identical word. A relative pronoun is (1) substituted for the identical element and (2) moved to a position next to the word that the clause modifies.

He gave his fortune to a country. He had never visited *this country.*

He gave his fortune to a country *which* he had never visited.

Make one sentence out of each of the following pairs of sentences, substituting a relative pronoun for the word in italics. Follow the example of the illustrative sentences from "An Unusual Bequest."

1. We discussed the incident. *It* was reported in the paper.
2. The report mentioned the professor. *He* taught the class in English conversation.
3. The incident concerned a carnival. The foreign students planned *the carnival.*

4. The student gave the story to the paper. The incident was reported to *the student*.
5. The paper has a very wide circulation. The story was reported *in the paper*.
6. The professor is very popular. The activities *of the professor* were discussed.
7. I wonder what the story said about this professor. I have heard so many good things about *this professor*.

▶ **Exercise 2**

Compare these two sentences:

A fellow *who scored 80 points last season* is our star basketball player.

Bill Clark, *who scored 80 points last season,* is our star basketball player.

In the first sentence, the clause identifies the boy. It is thus necessary for the meaning of the main clause of the sentence. Such a relative clause is called a *restrictive clause*. In the second sentence, the clause gives additional information about a person who has already been identified. Such a clause is called *nonrestrictive*. Commas precede and follow such clauses to indicate they might be omitted.

A similar contrast between restrictive and nonrestrictive clauses can be seen in these pairs of sentences adapted from the selection "An Unusual Bequest":

Most of the persons *who visit the Smithsonian* are unaware (no commas used)

Its founder was James Smithson, *an Englishman, who bequeathed his fortune* (commas required)

A. In the following passage, identify the relative clauses and tell why commas are or are not used to separate each one from the sentence in which it occurs.

Hawaii

In 1959 the territory of Hawaii, which consists of eight principal islands, became the fiftieth state of the United States. According to legend, the islands, which were visited in 1778 by Captain James Cook of the British navy, were settled many, many years ago by Polynesian people from Tahiti, who sailed across the Pacific in their large canoes. In the 1820s Protestant missionaries from New England, by whom the islands were Christianized, were followed by other Americans who came to develop businesses. Sugar and pineapple, which are the major industries of the island, formed the basis of fortunes for a number of these men. The Chinese and Japanese, who were also interested in jobs and in trade, also came in large numbers, and the islands have a mixed population of Asian, Polynesian, and European-American people. The beach of Waikiki, whose rolling surf attracts thousands of bathers, the sunny climate that shows little variation from day to day, and the beauty of the flowers that grow in profusion in the islands make Hawaii a place popular with vacationists, who believe the islands deserve the title "Paradise of the Pacific."

B. Applying the principles that you have just learned, add any necessary punctuation to the following paragraph.

Some Animal and Insect Traits

A subject which is very interesting is the study of the peculiar traits of some animals and insects. A horned grebe which is a species of bird feeds her babies feathers. Koala bears eat eucalyptus leaves which furnish all the moisture that their bodies need; therefore the bears never drink. They are the only mammals that do not. A woodcock has a long bill that looks like a pencil and that can be inserted into the burrows of worms which the woodcock eats. The jaçana bird which is found in the tropics of America has spurs that unfold like a razor blade and that the jaçana uses to kill its enemies. The two-headed skink whose tail looks exactly like his head confuses his enemy. When a hawk that is pursuing him thinks that the skink is going to run one way he runs another. The May fly which has no mouth lives only one happy day. These are just a few of the many interesting creatures that live in the world around us.

Verbals as Modifiers

The selection "An Unusual Bequest" also contains present participles, past participles, and infinitive constructions as modifiers.

Present participles

These are reductions of relative clauses with the verb in the active voice. Compare these pairs of structures:

> a warship *dating from the time of the American Revolution*
>
> a warship *which dates from the time of the American Revolution*

> The National Gallery of Art, *containing priceless paintings from all over the world.* . . .
>
> The National Gallery of Art, *which contains priceless paintings from all over the world.* . . .

Note that, like clauses, these participial constructions may be either restrictive (identifying) or nonrestrictive (interrupting the sentence pattern to give further information).

Past participles

These are reductions of relative clauses with the verb in the passive voice. Compare these pairs of sentence fragments:

> a collection *valued at more than a billion dollars* . . .
>
> a collection *that is valued at more than a billion dollars* . . .

> *impressed by the work of the British Royal Institution,* . . . he stated in his will . . .
>
> James Smithson, *who was impressed by the work of the British Royal Institution,* stated . . .

These constructions may also be restrictive or nonrestrictive, as indicated by the use of commas.

Infinitives

These are also reductions of relative clauses in the active voice.

Compare:

> the first spaceship *to go to the moon*
>
> the first spaceship *that went to the moon*

► **Exercise 3**

In the selection "An Unusual Bequest" find the following examples:

1. Two additional examples of present participles as modifiers.
2. Two additional examples of past participles as modifiers.
3. One more example of an appositive construction similar to "James Smithson, *an Englishman*." (The appositive *an Englishman* gives further information about James Smithson.)

► **Exercise 4**

Some of the following word groups with verbals are complete sentences. Some are not. Put a check mark in front of those that are sentences, and punctuate them correctly. Using the preceding patterns as a guide, complete those that are not and punctuate them correctly. Note that some of the sentences may be completed in more than one way.

1. The water dripping from the roofs _____
2. The speaker interested me in his subject _____
3. The lecture interesting to those who want jobs _____
4. The table covered with a yellow cloth _____
5. A yellow cloth covered the table _____
6. My friend seen all of those exhibits _____
7. The helicopter is hovering over us _____
8. An item listed in the paper _____
9. A professor giving a lecture _____
10. The professor given a good lecture _____
11. The work begun none too soon _____
12. The work has been done excellently _____
13. That man listening to me _____
14. That fellow to go to the farm with me _____
15. They were known as good fellows _____

► **Exercise 5**

In the following sentences, convert the relative clause into a verbal construction modifying a noun.

Examples
The instructions *that are typed on blue paper* will tell you how to assemble the machine.

The instructions *typed on blue paper* will tell you how to assemble the machine.

1. The plane *that is arriving at the airport* will bring guests from overseas.
2. One of the guests is an agronomist *who is famed for his work in developing new methods of agriculture.*
3. He will visit universities where experiments *that are performed under scientific conditions* have been undertaken.
4. He will tell us of methods *that are used in his country.*
5. His wife is a teacher *who is skilled in working with preschool children.*
6. She will give a lecture *that is designed to acquaint teachers with new methods.*
7. I hope to read her book *that gives further information about her procedures.*

▶ **Exercise 6**

To test your understanding of the use of present participles (v + –*ing*) and past participles (v + –*ed*, –*en*) as modifiers of nouns, read the following sentences aloud, supplying the correct participial forms.

Example
A girl who interests others is an *interesting* girl.
A girl who is interested by something is an *interested* girl.

1. A person who surprises others is a _____ person.
2. A person who is surprised by something is a _____ person.
3. A museum that intrigues someone is an _____ museum.
4. A lesson that confuses someone is a _____ lesson.
5. A noise that disturbs someone is a _____ noise.
6. Milk that someone spills is _____ milk.
7. A worker who is exhausted by a job is an _____ worker.

▶ **Exercise 7**

An infinitive or infinitive construction as a modifier of a noun may serve the same function as a clause but is more economical of words.

Compare:

That's a problem { that we must conquer soon. / to conquer soon (to be conquered soon). }

A thing { that you must remember / to remember (to be remembered) } is that he has always helped us.

The infinitive as a modifier indicates that something will be done (must be done) in the future. The passive infinitive (*to be remembered*) indicates permanent condition.

Following the pattern just given, change the italic clause modifiers in the following sentences to infinitive modifiers.

1. I have a good many things *that I must do* this afternoon.
2. Is there a deadline *that you must meet* in getting the work done?
3. The article *that has to be written* must be completed by Friday.
4. Is the material *that must be collected* for the article difficult to find?
5. Most of the articles *that I can find* on the subject are out of date. (Note that the passive infinitive must be used here. The speaker has already found the articles. The action is not projected to the future.)
6. Is there much *that you must do* before you write that article?
7. I would like to find a good book *that I can read* about the subject.

▶ **Exercise 8**

Clauses and verbal constructions as modifiers help indicate the precise relationship between ideas, and they make statements less wordy. Rewrite the following selection, expressing in one sentence the ideas between the bars. You will use clauses and verbal modifiers to do so.

At the Airport

/At the airport I always like to conjecture about the people while I am waiting for a plane. I see many people at the airport./ That man is a grandfather. He is standing beside a toy counter. He is meeting a plane. His daughter and two small grandchildren are arriving on the plane./ That couple are newly married. I can tell this because they are paying a great deal of attention to each other and look very happy. They are weighing in their luggage./ That man seems very nervous. He is behind them. He constantly checks his watch. He keeps listening intently to the loudspeaker. The loudspeaker announces the flights./ Perhaps he has missed an important appointment. He is trying to get to his destination. He will leave on the next plane./ That man is a business executive. He is wearing a dark suit./ Perhaps he is making a trip to Washington, D.C. He wants to talk to senators. The senators can initiate legislation. The legislation will help his business.

▶ **Exercise 9**

To give you practice in using the types of structure patterns in the selection "An Unusual Bequest," answer in complete sentences the following questions based on it. Underline verbal constructions and relative clauses that you use as modifiers. After you have answered the questions, check your answers with the original. Have you used structures correctly?

1. In what two ways is the Smithsonian Institution an unusual organization?
2. Illustrate how the transportation exhibit reflects the growth and development of the country.
3. How large is one of the locomotives in the collection?
4. What are three things that one may see in the display of objects associated with presidents?
5. What other kinds of exhibits can one see in the Smithsonian?
6. What are most of the visitors to the Smithsonian unaware of?
7. Who was James Smithson? Tell one fact about him.
8. What was unusual about the bequest of James Smithson?
9. After having accepted the gift, what did Congress set about doing?
10. Who was appointed the first secretary, and what had he done for science?

Composition

Write a composition of two to four paragraphs on one of the following:

An interesting institution in your country

A museum in your country

A national monument in your country

A sport in your country

In your first paragraph give some general facts about the subject to arouse interest, as is done in the selection "An Unusual Bequest." State your thesis sentence in the last sentence of the first paragraph. The thesis sentence should indicate that there are two (or three) things in particular that are interesting, unusual, exciting, or strange about your subject. (Note the last sentence in the first paragraph of "An Unusual Bequest.")

In the second paragraph describe one of the aspects that you have pointed out in your thesis sentence. In the third paragraph, describe the second one. If you have named three, describe the third in the fourth paragraph. End with a sentence that sums up what you have been discussing. Note the concluding sentence of "An Unusual Bequest."

In your presentation, use relative clauses and verbal constructions to give information and to describe. Underline these structures.

Before you start to write, make a list of the terms you are going to use.

Examples

this collection, valued at a million dollars,

the monument, which was constructed many years ago,

the person who first discovered it

a sport enjoyed by everyone

a picture representing a scene from history

Using Verbals and Clauses as Nouns: Showing Relationships Between Clauses and Sentences

Verbals as Subjects and Objects, Adverbial Structures; Subordinators and Sentence Connectors

PASSAGE FOR STUDY

Language and Culture

To know a person's language is to understand his culture, for language grows out of and reflects culture. The Tzeltal tribe in Mexico, for instance, has twenty-five different words for expressing the idea *to carry*. Tzeltal speakers can indicate by one word each of these concepts: carrying on the shoulder, carrying on the head, carrying in a bundle, carrying in the palm of the hand, or carrying in a container. To carry rolled up is expressed by *bal;* to carry coiled up is *ch'et;* to carry with tongs is *lut*. We know from his language that the Tzeltal does a lot of carrying.

Living halfway around the globe from the Tzeltal tribe are the Lapps in northern Sweden. The basis of the special Lapp culture is the reindeer, used as a beast of burden, as a draft animal, and for milking and slaughtering. The reindeer herd is called *aello,* meaning *what one lives on*. Because of the importance of the reindeer, about a quarter of the vocabulary in central Lappish has to do with reindeer breeding. There are a great many names for the reindeer, starting with certain words for the animal's basic appearance and age, the shape of its antlers, its color, and the various shades of its fur, its size, sex, and inner qualities. For instance, the Lapps give the male reindeer a different name each year until it is seven years old. The same discriminating differentiation is apparent in the vocabulary for all kinds of weather and the state of the snow in Lappish. Because snow conditions affect the reindeer pasture, the language has a finely shaded vocabulary for different kinds of snow covering. Thus the importance of reindeer in the culture is revealed in the Lapp language—in everyday speech, in song, and in legend.

The Tzeltal and Lapp languages thus inform us about the life of the people. Other cultures contain other examples of how language reflects what the people do and what they think about. Each of us might learn a lot about the environment in which we grew up by examining our own language.

Infinitive and Participial Constructions as Nouns

Infinitive constructions

Infinitives or infinitive constructions may function as the noun element in a sentence pattern. Note the following examples from the selection "Language and Culture":

SUBJECT   SUBJECTIVE COMPLEMENT

To know a person's language is *to understand his culture.*

Participial constructions

Forms ending in *–ing* may also be used as nouns. Such forms are called gerunds. Note the following examples:

SUBJECT

Carrying on the shoulder is one of the concepts.

OBJECT
OF PREP.

The Tzeltal does a lot of *carrying.*

▶ **Exercise 1**

Explain the function of each of the italicized verbals or verbal constructions in the following sentences. Is it used as a subject, an object, a complement, a modifier of a noun, or an adverbial?

1. *To carry rolled up* is expressed by *bal.*
2. Each of us might learn a lot about the environment in which we grew up by *examining our own language.*
3. The reindeer herd is called *aello,* meaning *what one lives on.*
4. The reindeer is used for *milking.*
5. A different word is used *to indicate every year of its age.*
6. Many words are used *to describe its characteristics.*
7. The same *discriminating* differentiation is apparent in the vocabulary for weather.
8. *Living halfway around the globe from the Tzeltal tribe* are the Lapps in northern Sweden.

▶ **Exercise 2**

Write a short paragraph about a vacation you might enjoy taking next summer, or during your next holiday period. Answer the following questions in your paragraph, using the indicated structures in your answers.

1. Where would you *enjoy going* on your vacation trip?
2. If it is impossible to go there, what might you *consider doing* as an alternative?
3. What or whom would you *appreciate having* with you?
4. What do you *look forward to seeing* on your vacation?
5. What would you like *having* (or *to have*) as a souvenir of your trip?
6. After your return what will you *remember doing* or *remember seeing* with the greatest pleasure?

▶ **Exercise 3**

Write a paragraph beginning:

One of my ambitions is to . . .

Use one of the following, or a similar construction, to complete the opening sentence:

to go to the moon
to live a peaceful life in today's world

to make a great scientific discovery
to become a millionaire
to learn to ice-skate
to live to be a hundred years old

Develop your paragraph with a few sentences telling why you would *like to* realize your particular ambition, when you *expect to* or *intend to* begin to do it, what you will *try to* do, or *learn to* do, or what you *mean to* do to attain your goal.

Note that certain verbs may be followed by an infinitive; others may be followed by a gerund. Some may be followed by either one. Consult the list on p. 234 of the Appendix. In your passage try to use a number of the verbs that can be followed by infinitives.

▶ **Exercise 4**

For practice in using verbs with infinitives or gerunds (*–ing* forms used as nouns) as complements, write a paragraph entitled "What My Parents Taught Me." Begin with the topic sentence:

I have learned many things from my parents.

Continue by completing the following statements as indicated:

My parents always taught me _____. (infinitive)
They urged me _____. (infinitive)
Sometimes they had to force me _____. (infinitive)
I was encouraged _____. (infinitive)
After warning me several times _____. (infinitive)
I often resisted _____. (gerund)
I always hated _____ (gerund or infinitive), but my parents insisted on my _____. (gerund)
They often had to remind me _____. (infinitive)
I often resented their _____ (gerund), and I would continue _____. (gerund)
But now that I am grown, I appreciate their _____. (gerund)

Conclude the paragraph with this sentence:

I see that their training was a big factor in my growing up.

Clauses as Nouns

Clauses introduced by *that* and *what* may be used as substitutes for nouns.

Compare:

We know from his language *that the Tzeltal does a lot of carrying.* (an assertion)

Language reflects *what the people do* and *what they think about.* (a conclusion)

Note the distinction between the use of *that* and *what*. *That* merely introduces the subordinate idea: *The Tzeltals do a lot of carrying.* It is not an element in the noun clause. *What* serves as a sentence element—the object of *do* (what the people *do*) and of the preposition *about* (what they think *about*).

▶ **Exercise 5**

Write a paragraph about a lecture you have heard, or an event you have witnessed, or a person you have known. Express an attitude toward your subject in your topic sentence. If possible, use four of the following in your paragraph, or use similar clauses as nouns. Underline the examples of clauses as nouns that you have used.

what he said	that caused the improvement
that I could go	what a remarkable event it was
that you agree	that I have always wanted
that it can be done	how he was able to be elected to office
what can be done	whatever success he has obtained

Noun Clauses Reduced to Infinitives

Note how noun clauses introduced by *what* or other interrogative words may be reduced to infinitives, particularly in stating instructions or directions.

Compare:

> He told me *what I should do.*
> He told me *what to do.*

Other examples of reductions are:

> *How to do* it was not clear.
> *Where to go* was our problem.
> They explained *where to go.*

▶ **Exercise 6**

Write on A or B.

A. Write a short account of an experience you have had in a situation that was new to you, when you did not know *what to do, where to go,* or *whom to ask.* Tell about matters that perplexed you.

Suggested topics:

> The first day on a new job
> A trip to a strange city
> A formal social occasion
> Shopping in a new place

Use as many of the constructions below as are appropriate, or similar ones. Underline them in your passage.

how to get there	whom to see
what to ask for	which to do first
when to come	where to go

B. Write a paragraph of advice for an inexperienced traveler in a foreign country. Use constructions suggested in the preceding exercise.

Markers of Relationships Between Clauses

Clauses may be inserted into a sentence pattern to modify a noun (adjectival clauses—Lesson 6), or to modify the verb or the entire sentence pattern (adverbial clauses). Adverbial clauses in "Language and Culture" are:

> *Because snow conditions affect the reindeer pasture,* the [Lapp] language has a finely shaded vocabulary for different kinds of snow covering. (The italicized element is an adverbial stating cause.)
>
> The Lapps give the male reindeer a different name each year *until it is seven years old.* (The italicized element is an adverbial stating time.)

The relationship of the adjectival clause to the main clause is shown by the relative pronoun (Lesson 6). The relationship of the adverbial clause is shown by the subordinating word (*because, until*). The adverbial clause, like the prepositional phrase, may show time, place, manner or purpose (Lesson 4), or it may show condition, contrast, comparison, or cause. For subordinating words and the relationships they indicate, see the Appendix, pp. 243–245. Some subordinate clauses may be reduced to prepositional phrases:

> *Because of the importance* of the reindeer, about a quarter of the vocabulary in central Lappish has to do with reindeer breeding.

► **Exercise 7**

A. Some of the following word groups are complete sentences and some are only long adverbial elements. For each word group that is not a complete sentence, complete the sentence with as few words as possible and punctuate it correctly. For each word group that is a complete sentence, put in the appropriate punctuation.

1. Once we agreed immediately upon a place to take our vacation
2. Once we have decided upon a place to take our vacation
3. Afterward we studied hard all semester and took our final examinations
4. After we have studied hard all semester and have taken our final examinations

5. Now that we have got through the annoying red tape of registration
6. Now we have learned how to get through the annoying red tape of registration
7. As soon as we can notify our parents
8. As soon as November we can notify our parents
9. While we were waiting Bill appeared at the corner
10. While we were waiting for Bill at the corner
11. For so long his family kept sending him a generous allowance
12. So long as his family keep sending him a generous allowance
13. Whenever possible I write my long term papers during vacation
14. Whenever I write my long term papers during vacation
15. Before he decided that law was the profession that most nearly suited him
16. Before he came he had decided that law was the profession that suited him

B. Rewrite sentences 2, 4, 5, 7, and 10, putting the long adverbial element in regular order at the end of the sentence. How will the punctuation of the sentences in this rewriting differ from the punctuation used in your first writing?

► **Exercise 8**

When the subject and verb of an included adverbial clause are clear, they are often omitted.

Example
Although (he was) tired he kept on working.

However, be careful that such an elliptical clause does not result in ambiguity or in a statement that is obviously false.

Example
When prepared, eat the soup. (Is the soup prepared, or is the eater?)

Rewrite the following sentences using the elliptical pattern that has just been explained, if the ellipsis will not result in ambiguity.

1. Even though he was in a hurry, the father took time to answer the child's question.

2. When he was ready to leave the hotel, the tourist called for some-one to carry his bags.
3. When the baby is bathed, please put the soap back where you found it.
4. Please remove the soup from the stove when it is done.
5. Although he was exhausted, the track star continued the race.
6. Although Harry Jones was the most industrious student, the committee awarded the prize to the writer of the best essay.
7. Although one musician was late, the concert began on time.
8. Although she was late, my aunt enjoyed the program.

▶ Exercise 9

Present or past participle constructions, with or without noun subjects, are often used adverbially at the beginning of a sentence to signify the conditions under which the action stated in the main pattern of the sentence occurred. These are sometimes called *absolute constructions*.

Examples
Having spent all our money, we went home for more.
Our program for the year finished, we took a vacation.

Complete sentences 1 through 5, telling what you think probably happened under the suggested conditions. Complete sentences 6 through 10 by telling what the conditions were under which each of the actions were performed. Follow the pattern at the beginning of this exercise.

1. His suit absolutely ruined, the professor _____.
2. Land having been sighted, the ship's crew _____.
3. Our car having run out of gas, we _____.
4. Hearing a strange noise, the burglar _____.
5. Having studied astronomy for three years, I _____.
6. _____, the professor immediately fainted.
7. _____, my roommate failed the examination.
8. _____, the club went on an outing.
9. _____, I voted for the other candidate.
10. _____, Mr. Smith decided to retire from business.

Markers of Sequence of Sentences

When the ideas expressed in two sentences are closely connected, the sentences are frequently put together into one sentence and linked by a conjunction—*and, but, or, nor, so,* and others.

Examples

It was late, *but* the guests had not arrived.

He told me that he did it, *and* I believed him.

Note the punctuation in the patterns just given.

Sentences may also be joined by sentence connectors (*therefore, consequently, however,* etc.), which indicate the relationship of ideas.

Note the placement of sentence connectors and the punctuation in the following sentences:

I went to the meeting; *however,* I did not stay very long.

I went to the meeting. I did not stay very long, *however.*

I went to the meeting. I did not, *however,* find out what I wanted to know.

But: We went to California last summer. We visited the Grand Canyon, too.

When sentences are linked by sentence connectors, a semicolon (;) is used between the sentence patterns, or each pattern may be punctuated as a sentence by itself. If the sentence connector is more than one syllable long, it is generally separated by a comma from the sentence pattern in which it occurs.

Sentence connectors indicate the addition or restatement of an idea, contrast of ideas, result, and sequence of time. For a summary of the uses of sentence connectors, see the Appendix, p. 248.

▶ **Exercise 10**

Join the following pairs of sentences into one sentence, using appropriate sentence connectors (not conjunctions). Put the sentence connector at the beginning of the second clause, and use suitable punctuation. When you have finished the exercise, rewrite the sentences, changing the position of the sentence connector and making necessary changes in punctuation.

1. It is raining. We will go to the meeting.
2. He passed the examination. He received his certificate.
3. One can make a great deal of money in that profession. The hours are long and the work difficult.
4. The assignment was very difficult. We did not finish it as soon as we had expected.
5. This is the most beautiful design of its kind that I have ever seen. It is the only one I have ever seen.
6. The city is famous for its art gallery. It has a fine symphony.
7. It was a very cold night. We decided to stay at home.
8. The competition is keen. You must work hard if you want to be successful.
9. The car ran out of gasoline. They had to remain there for the night.
10. He does the work very slowly. He usually does it well.

▶ **Exercise 11**

A. Note how paragraph 2 in the following selection is made more vivid and more unified by the use of conjunctions and sentence connectors to show the relationship of the ideas.

Concord, Massachusetts

(1) The small town of Concord, Massachusetts, has played an important part in American political history. It has played an important part in American literary history. It was through the towns of Concord and Lexington that the British soldiers marched in 1775 to keep the rebellious colonists under control. It was at the old stone bridge in Concord that the first battle of the American Revolution took place. In the early part of the nineteenth century, Concord was the home of a group of American writers and philosophers. It became a center of literary activity. Ralph Waldo Emerson, the poet, essayist, and Transcendentalist philosopher, made Concord his home. For a time the novelist Nathaniel Hawthorne lived there. Henry David Thoreau was a resident of Concord. Thoreau is known for his book *Walden,* an account of his life in the woods. He is known for his essay "Civil Disobedience." This essay reflects

Thoreau's opposition to slavery. In brief, this quiet, charming New England town has figured importantly in the development of the American nation. Many tourists visit it each year.

(2) The small town of Concord, Massachusetts, has played an important role *not only* in American political history but in American literary history *as well*. It was through the towns of Lexington and Concord that the British soldiers marched in 1775 to keep the rebellious colonists under control, *and consequently* it was at the old stone bridge in Concord that the first battle of the American Revolution took place. *Moreover,* in the early part of the nineteenth century, Concord was the home of a group of writers and philosophers, and *therefore* became a center of literary activity. Ralph Waldo Emerson, the poet, essayist, and Transcendentalist philosopher, made Concord his home, and for a time *so did* the novelist Nathaniel Hawthorne. Henry David Thoreau was *also* a resident of Concord. Thoreau is known *not only* for his book *Walden,* an account of his life in the woods, *but also* for his essay "Civil Disobedience" which reflects Thoreau's opposition to slavery. In brief, this quiet, charming New England town has *thus* figured importantly in the development of the American nation. *Therefore,* many tourists visit it each year.

B. Read paragraph 2 aloud, substituting other appropriate conjunctions and sentence connectors for those that have been used.

▶ **Exercise 12**

Rewrite the following passage, adding conjunctions to show addition, contrast, comparison, or result, as has been done in paragraph 2 of the preceding exercise.

California Gold

In 1849 gold was discovered in California. Many people went there to seek their fortunes. A great migration to the West was begun. People moved into California in large numbers. Some towns doubled in population almost overnight. Buildings were hastily constructed. They were not built to last. As the gold mines were exhausted, the settlements became "ghost towns." The Wild West in those days was a place of excitement, glamour, danger, and lawlessness. Later permanent settlements were made. A few of the "forty-niners," as these early settlers were called, made the fortunes in gold they had come to seek. Others made more modest fortunes in merchandising or farming or ranching. Still others returned home, as poor as when they had left.

▶ **Exercise 13**

So that as a subordinator indicating a planned purpose is often confused with *so* as a conjunction indicating result.

Compare:

> Jack pretended to be ill *so that* he would not have to take the examination. (purpose—he pretended illness *because* he did not want to take the examination)
> Jack was ill, *so* (or *therefore*) he missed the examination. (an unplanned consequence)

Complete each of the following sentences in two ways: first, with a clause with *so that* to show planned purpose and, second, with a clause using *so* to indicate an unplanned result. The first one is done for you.

1. Miss Thompson brushes her teeth three times a day,
    a. so that she won't get cavities.
    b. so she buys a lot of toothpaste.
2. John bought four pens _____.
3. Jim is wearing his old clothes in the rain _____.
4. Mr. Jones parked his car near the store _____.
5. The political candidate gave many speeches _____.

Composition

Write a composition with this as the topic sentence:

An inexperienced person encounters a great many difficulties in *applying for a job.*

You may want to write about some activity other than the one in italics. Choose your own, or select one of the following:

Suggestions:

Giving a talk

Apologizing for a mistake

Asking a girl for the first date

Explaining directions to one who neither speaks nor understands your language well

Trying to start a car on a cold morning

Washing a dog

Trying to soothe a terrified child

Surviving during a crisis caused by nature (hurricane, sandstorm, flood, snowstorm, fire, etc.)

Keeping calm during a dramatic moment in your life (a graduation; first communion; marriage ceremony; your first public performance in speaking, acting, or playing a musical instrument; some responsibility assigned to you by your parents or a teacher when you were very young; an exciting athletic contest)

Registering and staying in a big hotel

Asking your father for something you know he will not approve of

Develop your proposition by explaining the aspect of the activity that is difficult. Note the use of examples in the selection "Language and Culture." Give examples or illustrations from your personal experience or the experience of people you have known. Underline the verbal structures you use.

Expressing Attitudes with Modals: A Further Word on Verbals *Uses of Modal Auxiliaries; Infinitives as Adverbials and as Complements of Adjectives*

PASSAGE FOR STUDY

Mesa Verde

Some day I would like to visit Mesa Verde, the high plateau, or "green table," which rises abruptly from the floor of a valley in the southwest corner of Colorado. Some of the oldest remains of human life on the North American continent can be found there. If I were there I could see ruins of cliff dwellings dating from the twelfth or thirteenth centuries. These are the best-preserved cliff dwellings in existence.

A visitor to Mesa Verde ought to know something of the history of the area to make his stay there more interesting. If a person visited the museum in the area he could learn something about people who once lived on the mesa. Scientists tell us that this region may have been inhabited since A.D. 500. The first inhabitants raised corn and squash on the table top and engaged in hunting in the valley below. Later groups had more sophisticated societies. From the year 750 to about 1200, the people in Mesa Verde lived in villages called pueblos, consisting of clay and stone houses built around a central court. The museum contains models where one can see the pueblo people carrying on their daily activities, and it is easy for the visitor to imagine what their life must have been like. Because they built their houses in an area protected by the high walls of the mesa, we can guess that they must have been afraid of hostile tribes. After 1200, the inhabitants of the pueblos moved into caves in the cliff walls. These dwellings, in spectacular defensive positions, are exceedingly difficult to get to, so we can suppose that the danger from enemies must have increased. It was not enemies, however, but drought that finally drove man from Mesa Verde, around the year 1273.

The visitor who explores the fifteen-to-twenty-mile extent of Mesa Verde on foot must take his hiking boots, but on a hot day he might prefer to tour the area in a "mini-train" provided by the National Park Service. A sight-seer might have to climb ladders to reach many of the ruins. To visit Balcony House, one of the more spectacular dwellings, he would have to climb a ladder thirty-two feet long—a difficult feat for some visitors to accomplish. Tourists may go to Balcony House only with a guide. One should also visit Cliff Palace, one of the largest of the cliff dwellings. Visitors may be surprised to find that it contains 200 rooms and rises four stories high. In it there are also thirty-two "kivas"—secret ceremonial shelters—to be explored. Unfortunately, because the structure is too weak to stand the weight of many people, it is impossible to visit Fire Palace. Its symmetrical construction and the absence of grinding tools lead scientists to believe that the structure was once used for ceremonial purposes. There is evidence that there once were paintings on the walls of this dwelling, and remains on well-made pottery are to be found throughout the area.

These cliff dwellings have aroused interest throughout the world, and one of the actual dwellings has been transported to the British Museum in London. I hope to make my trip to Mesa Verde very soon, to see for myself how the earliest men in North America lived.

Modals

The selection "Mesa Verde" illustrates how auxiliary verbs called modals are used with the simple form of the verb to express hypothetical conditions and conjectures as well as attitudes such as willingness, ability, permission, possibility, advisability, obligation, and necessity. Detailed uses of modals are given in the Appendix, pp. 236–241. Some of the more common uses are summarized here, with examples adapted from the selection, when possible.

Attitudes

Desire—*would*

> I *would* like to visit Mesa Verde

Willingness—*will, would*

> I *will* go if you ask me.
> I *would* go if you asked me.

Ability—*can, could*

> Some of the oldest remains of human life *can* be found [at Mesa Verde].
> If I were there I *could* see ruins of cliff dwellings. (Note the use of *were* as a subjunctive form in the expression of a hypothetical condition.)

Possibility—*may, might*

> This region *may* have been inhabited since A.D. 500.
> Visitors *might* prefer to tour the area by "mini-train." (In these sentences *may* and *might* are interchangeable.)

Advisability—*shall* (used in questions—see Lesson 3)

> *Shall* we visit Mesa Verde?

Obligation—*should, ought to*

> One *should* also visit Cliff Palace.
> A visitor to Mesa Verde *ought to* know something of the history of the area.

Should and *ought to* indicate recognition of obligation but not necessarily intention to fulfill the obligation.

Compare:

> I *should* (*ought to*) study tonight, but I guess I'll go to the movies.
> I can't go to the movies tonight. I *must* (*have to*) study.

Necessity—*must, have to*

The visitor who explores [the area] on foot *must* take his hiking boots. . . .

Note the difference between *must not* and *don't have to:*

Must not indicates prohibition.

Don't have to indicates lack of necessity.

Examples

You *must not* drive 80 miles an hour. It is illegal. (prohibition)

You *do not have to* drive so fast. We have plenty of time. (lack of necessity)

Conjecture—*must be, must have*

These *must be* interesting ruins, because many people visit them.

The danger from enemies *must have* increased.

Hypothetical Conditions

The past tense forms—*could, would, might, should,* and *must*—express hypothetical conditions.

If I were there, I *could* see the ruins.

I *would* go if I could.

You *ought to* visit Mesa Verde.

You *should see* Cliff Palace.

They *must have* been afraid of hostile tribes.

▶ **Exercise 1**

Suppose that you have accepted a part-time job while you are going to school. Explain to another person how you could adjust your working hours to your class schedule, how you could get transportation to the job, how you could utilize your abilities in the job, and what you could do with the money you would get from it. Use as your topic sentence:

I think I could adjust to a part-time job while I am going to school.

▶ Exercise 2

Note the difference in the sequence of tenses when the statements refer to present or past time.

If I *understood* him, I *would answer.*
If I *had understood* him, I *would have answered.*

Tell what you would do under each of the following conditions. Begin your sentences as indicated.

1. If I were a millionaire, I _____.
2. If I could speak ten languages, I _____.
3. If I lived in a cold country, I _____.
4. If I lived in a hot country, I _____.
5. If I had 17 children, I _____.
6. If I were famous, I _____.
7. If we had known that there would be a test, _____.
8. If I had not opened the door, _____.
9. If the professor had arrived earlier, _____.
10. If I had only studied the lesson, _____.

▶ Exercise 3

The following sentences begin a paragraph that you are asked to complete by giving further examples.

Routine Work

People in responsible jobs generally have to perform some routine tasks each day. A nurse in a large hospital has to fill out temperature and pulse charts. Any executive receives a certain amount of correspondence that he must take care of. A teacher has to . . .

▶ Exercise 4

Note the use of *must not* to express prohibition. Suppose there has been a disaster in your town—an earthquake, flood, or fire. You are temporary mayor. In order to maintain law and order and keep the people alive and well, issue four statements about things they must or must not do. Make at least one of the statements negative.

▶ Exercise 5

Write a short paragraph that starts in the following fashion:

Vacations release students from tiresome routine. During a vacation students do not have to go to class.

Add four other examples of things that students do not have to do.

▶ Exercise 6

As we have seen earlier in this lesson, *must* indicates a necessity or an obligation which the speaker intends to fulfill. *Should* indicates an obligation which is recognized, but which the speaker does not necessarily intend to fulfill. Write a paragraph five or six sentences long, beginning:

I have a lot of things to do today.

Name two or three things that you *must* do. Then tell of some things that you *should* do but probably will not. You might mention some of the following:

write a letter   go to bed early
go to the doctor   return a book to the library
speak English   pick up some theater tickets

▶ Exercise 7

In the following sentences note the use of *must* to express inference:

1. There are five daily newspapers on the neighbors' front porch. The family *must be* away from home.
2. John has worked hard all day. He *must* feel tired.
3. The dog is barking at the door. He *must* want to get in.

Using the pattern of these sentences, write sentences telling what you infer from each of the following. The word in parentheses provides a cue.

1. The car won't start. (gasoline)
2. Bill didn't come to class today. (ill)

3. The newspaper hasn't arrived yet. (newsboy)
4. The bell for classes did not ring this morning. (out of order)
5. John is afraid to walk past the old house at midnight. (ghosts)
6. Henry squints when he reads. (eyesight)
7. There goes a fire engine. (fire)
8. Tom reads that book repeatedly. (like)
9. That woman is running across the campus. (late)
10. He almost lives in the library. (graduate student)

Infinitive Constructions as Adverbials and as Complements of Adjectives

The selection "Mesa Verde" contains uses of infinitives that have not been noted in detail in previous lessons, as follows:

A. Infinitives can be used as adverbials to express purpose or reason.

A visitor to Mesa Verde ought to know something of the history of the area *to make* his stay there more interesting.

This use was noted in Lesson 4.

B. Infinitive constructions can be used after adjectives that are inversions of sentences with infinitive constructions as subjects. These constructions appear after adjectives.

Other patterns with infinitive constructions in this lesson may best be understood as inversions of sentences with infinitive constructions as subjects.

Compare:

To visit this high plateau would be interesting.
It would be interesting *to visit this high plateau.* (inversion)

Others are more complicated.

Compare:

It is easy *for the visitor to imagine what their life must have been like.*
To imagine what their life must have been like is easy for the visitor.

The visitor can easily imagine what their life must have been like.

Compare also:

It is a difficult feat *for some visitors to accomplish.*
To accomplish this feat is difficult for some people.
Some people accomplish this feat with difficulty.

The pattern with *It is*–adjective–infinitive, or *It is*–noun–prepositional phrase–infinitive follows Sentence Pattern 6c in Lesson 1. Such sentences are inverted sentences with the "dummy subject" *it*. This pattern may not be found in other languages with which you are familiar.

▶ **Exercise 8**

A. Use *too* + adjective + infinitive constructions to describe each of the following:

1. someone you like

Example
My roommate is *too intelligent to fail* the examination.

2. someone you do not like
3. a pet that you have
4. an article of clothing that you own
5. an assignment to which you object

B. A similar construction may be used with *enough.*

Example
He is *old enough to know* better.

Use this pattern in an advertising slogan for each of the following. The first one is done for you.

1. soap (gentle)

This soap is *gentle enough to make* your skin soft as a baby's.

2. an automobile (fast)
3. house paint (durable)

4. a dress (pretty)
5. wine (old)
6. pencil (sharp)

▶ **Exercise 9**

Write sentences describing each of the following people when they did the thing indicated. Follow this pattern:

In the middle of the night I *was frightened to hear* a loud noise.

1. The professor _____ receive a present from his students.
2. The scientist _____ make a great discovery.
3. The class _____ see the professor stand on his head.
4. Alexander the Great _____ conquer the world.
5. Napoleon _____ fight the Battle of Waterloo.

▶ **Exercise 10**

To review the structures in the selection "Mesa Verde" that are studied in this lesson, answer *in complete sentences* these questions based on it. In each answer use the structure underlined in the question.

1. What *would the author like* to do some day?
2. What does the author think that *it would be interesting* to see at Mesa Verde?
3. If a person visited the museum, what *would it be possible to learn?*
4. What do you think the visitor *ought to know* before going to Mesa Verde?
5. Why is it *easy for the visitor to imagine* what the life of the pueblo people *must have been* like?
6. Because they built their houses on a high mesa, what can we guess *must have been* one of their fears?
7. What would the tourist *have to do to visit* some of the more spectacular ruins?
8. What *may be* a difficult feat *for some visitors to accomplish?*
9. Why *is it impossible to visit* Fire Palace?
10. What is *to be found* throughout the area?

Composition

Write on A or B.

A. Write a composition beginning:

Someday I would like to visit (place).

or

Someday you ought to visit (place).

Choose a place of interest that you know something about. In your first paragraph tell about some of the things a visitor *ought to,* or *must,* or *should* know about the place before going there, as was done in the selection "Mesa Verde." In the second paragraph tell of some of the things it would be *interesting to see* or *important* for the visitor *to see* once he is there. Use as many modals and infinitive constructions as are appropriate. In a summary paragraph give an example, if possible, that illustrates the popularity of the place, as in the concluding paragraph of "Mesa Verde."

B. Write a composition in which you conjecture what life might be like if you were one of the following:

a teacher	a person who can	an engineer
a priest	speak five languages	a leader in your country
a doctor	an airplane pilot	(or any other type of per-
an astronaut	or hostess	son that you would
an architect	a farmer	like to be)
	a scientist	

Your opening sentence might be:

I have often thought that I would like to be (a person mentioned in the preceding list).

In your first paragraph tell what you *ought to* know or do or *should* know or do or *would have to* know or do if you were this person. In your second paragraph tell what a typical day might be like. In your concluding paragraph you might give a specific reason why you would enjoy being this particular type of person.

PART TWO
Writing
in Rhetorical Patterns

Writing the Longer Composition
An Overview

At this point in your study of writing English, you will advance from directed, or controlled, writing to free expression of your ideas. You will be choosing topics and developing and arranging your material without the specific directions that guided your paragraph writing in Part I of this book. Because writing is an art, you will now learn the vocabulary, the principles, and the techniques of that art in a systematic way. Principles that you have used in Part I through intuition or by direction will be discussed so that you can have conscious control of your means of expression and thus be more certain of the quality of the writing that you do.

Read the following essays, which will give you an overview of the content of and the rationale for the lessons in Part II of this text. After reading each essay, answer the questions that follow it.

PASSAGE FOR STUDY

> *Rhetoric: What Is It and Why Study It?*

(1) Because the art of writing is much more than a matter of writing correct sentences, Part II of this textbook deals with rhetoric. The term *rhetoric* has several quite different meanings that are used in different contexts, so let us examine what the word means as we use it here and what purposes rhetoric fulfills.

(2) Just as art students study proportion and balance and musicians study harmony, so writers are concerned with principles

of handling ideas in order that what they write will be more interesting, will be clearer, and will be more persuasive. It is this body of principles, based on observation and analysis of language for generations, that we call rhetoric. In order to understand what rhetoric is and why it is important for writers to study it, let us begin with a brief history of the art.

(3) On the island of Corsica, in ancient times, a tyrant seized power and took the land away from the common people, who had traditionally owned their homes and farms. Eventually the descendants of the tyrant were overthrown, and one of the reforms of the new government was to return the land to private ownership. But after several generations, everyone had forgotten what families owned what land. Courts, therefore, were set up so that an individual could come before the judge; if he could persuade the judge that his family had once owned a specific parcel of land, the judge would award the land to him. As one could predict, the individual who could speak most persuasively got the land he wanted, whether or not his family had actually owned it previously. Onlookers with an eye for business sat in the courts day after day and observed what types of argument seemed to be the most effective in persuading the judge. Then, for a fee, they went out and taught would-be owners of land how to argue their cases.

(4) The art of persuasion was nurtured further in the Greek city-states 2500 years ago. Since these states were democracies, laws advocated by the most eloquent speaker in the forum were passed, and citizens who could speak most persuasively before the judges won their cases. It became highly important in this society for a man to know how to select and express his ideas, so the Greeks gave a great deal of thought to just what kinds of arguments influence other people.

(5) Today, rhetoric is more than a study of the principles of persuasion. In the practical affairs of life—in business, in school, in research, in the various professions—people need to know how to inform other people. They need to know how to give clear instructions, to outline a plan of procedure, to write proposals and recommendations; they need to be able to summarize, interpret, evaluate, describe a process or the results of a process. Thus the art of rhetoric still flourishes, but the emphasis in schools today is on the principles of exposition.

(6) A second difference between the function of rhetoric in ancient and in modern times is that now the number of *writing* classes that study rhetoric exceeds the number of speech classes in

which it is studied. The printing press has made writing a universal form of communication; and as students reach higher and higher levels of education, they are required to write in an increasingly skillful way. The writing of essay examinations or term papers and the preparation of theses and dissertations demand skill that can be learned most efficiently through a study of rhetoric.

(7) Until now we have been speaking about how a body of knowledge we call rhetoric has developed, and we have seen in a very general way what it is intended to do. Let us now take a closer look at rhetoric to see exactly what matters it is concerned with. Perhaps a comparison with the art of architectural engineering will give us a clearer picture. When an architect is asked to construct a building, there are certain important facts that he needs to know before he can start. He needs to know whether he is to draw plans for a home, an office building, an apartment complex, or an airport. He also needs to know whether the client has personal preferences in the style of building he wants erected. Of course the architect needs to know, too, about how much money the client intends to spend. Then the architect and client may also discuss legal regulations.

(8) Similarly, there are certain things that a writer must take into account before he puts pen to paper. He needs to know whether he is trying to persuade his reader, to inform him, or to entertain him. He needs to know whether the reader is well educated, whether he is interested in the subject, and to what extent he is knowledgeable about it. The writer has to know the approximate length of what he is going to write. He needs also to consider which of several possible patterns of arrangement of ideas would be most effective.

(9) The following chart shows the similarity between the things that the architect and the writer must consider before they begin to work.

Architect	Writer
1. Purpose of the building (dwelling, airport terminal)	1. Purpose of the writing (to persuade, to inform, to entertain)
2. Characteristics of the client (does not like modern buildings)	2. Characteristics of the reader (well educated, knowledgeable about subject, interested in it)
3. Money available for the building (minimal or unrestricted)	3. Length of the writing (600 words? 15,000 words?)
4. Building design as affected by certain requirements	4. Writing design as affected by the expectations and attitudes of the reader

(10) There is yet another important area of concern that is common to the architect and to the writer. Each has the responsibility not only for the overall structure of the product but for the selection of the materials of which the product is to be made. The architect and the writer must choose materials that suit the purpose; and the wider the range of materials each has to choose from, the better the finished product will be.

(11) It cannot be overemphasized that choosing the kinds of material from which to build is quite a different matter from designing the overall structure. In writing we refer to the selection of material as *the development of ideas*. This is what the writer does when he tries to answer these questions that the reader might ask: What do you mean? How do you know? Why do you think that?

(12) Planning the overall structure in writing is called *organization*. Here the writer considers what he will present first and what last, and how he will arrange what is in between. It is quite possible for the overall organization to be excellent, but for the development of ideas to be ineffective. It is also possible for a writer to have superb materials (or development of ideas) and yet present them in such a fashion that the reader finds it difficult to follow the overall train of thought.

(13) In summary, the study of rhetoric is a study of ways to develop and arrange ideas in order to achieve the writer's purpose. Such study develops in the writer a sense of awareness of the reader: the questions the reader asks as he reads and his problems in following the writer's thinking. *Rhetorical techniques can be thought of as providing options rather than prescribing behavior.*

(14) As an individual is called upon to write upon more and more challenging subjects and has more discriminating and critical readers, it becomes more important to study rhetorical principles. Such study is important for writing in one's native language, and even more important when one writes in a foreign language.

▶ **Exercise 1**

Circle the letter preceding the answer that best completes each of the following sentences:

1. The word *rhetoric,* as used in this text, means
   a. prose as opposed to poetry.
   b. the art of influencing thought and conduct.

c. the art of developing and arranging ideas.

d. the art of using words.

2. The principles of rhetoric began to be observed

a. a hundred years ago.

b. 2500 years ago in Greece.

c. after the invention of the printing press.

d. in ancient times in Corsica.

3. The principles of rhetoric were first observed

a. by grammarians.

b. by lawyers.

c. in order to earn money.

d. in order to help student compositions.

4. Rhetoric began as a study of

a. persuasion.

b. exposition.

c. description.

d. narration.

5. Today rhetoric might be studied by students of

a. advanced reading.

b. public speaking.

c. writing.

d. reading, public speaking, and writing.

▶ **Exercise 2**

In order to study the patterns of organization in the passage that you have just read, answer these questions:

1. Which is the better purpose sentence for this essay—the last sentence in paragraph 1 or the last sentence in paragraph 2? Explain.

2. Why can the history of rhetoric as given here be considered a part of the body of the essay and not just a lengthy introduction? (The title and the purpose sentence will help to guide your answer.)

3. The first section on history is organized chronologically—that is, by time. First the writer tells us of the use of rhetoric in ancient times on the island of Corsica. The next paragraph discusses a later period, the time of the Greek city-states 2500 years

ago. What period of time is discussed in the next paragraph? How does this represent a consistent plan of organization?

4. Paragraph 7 begins the second section of the essay. What sentence states the purpose of this section? What sentence forms a transition between the first section of the essay and the second?

5. The second section of the essay discusses two points. The first is that rhetoric is concerned with organization (or structure) of a piece of writing. What is the second point of the essay? (See paragraph 10.)

6. Find the place where the writer summarizes what he has said. What words indicate that he has arrived at the concluding part of his essay?

▶ **Exercise 3**

1. At what stage in writing do you think a knowledge of rhetoric would be most useful—planning, writing, or revision? Give the reason for your answer.

2. Why is the writing of novels, plays, and poetry not so widely taught as the writing of expository prose?

3. What important principles of writing have you been taught?

4. Do you think most of the principles of rhetoric have been arrived at through trial and error or by calculated reasoning? (You can safely base your answer on the experience of ancient people.)

5. Why has the emphasis in rhetoric changed from the means of persuasion to the means of exposition?

6. What opportunities for giving information do you encounter in your daily life (at home, in social situations, in school)? What opportunities for persuasion do you have? When you explain reasons, are you dealing in exposition or persuasion?

PASSAGE FOR STUDY

Rhetoric Across Cultures

(1) We all expect to encounter different sounds when we learn a new language, and we are not surprised to find differences in grammar and vocabulary between our first language and those

languages we acquire later. But for some reason we know less about rhetorical habits in other cultures.

(2) It is not that the basic patterns of reasoning are different. People around the world engage in *inductive reasoning*. For example, they would all conclude, on the basis of the limited number of men whom they have known or heard about or read about, that all men are mortal. Universally, minds take this inductive leap. Induction is a very necessary kind of thought. Statements of conclusions arrived at by this method—for example, "Fires are hot," "Knives can cut," "Oranges contain vitamins"—are called *generalizations;* they help us to accommodate to the world we live in.

(3) Inductive reasoning also serves as a basis for another kind of thought: *deductive reasoning*. People constantly say things such as, "John Brown would make a good town mayor." Behind such a statement is this train of thought:

Major premise: Good town mayors are astute businessmen, public spirited, and honest.
Minor premise: John Brown is an astute businessman, public spirited, and honest.
Conclusion: John Brown would make a good mayor

The major premise and minor premise are conclusions arrived at through inductive reasoning. When we put two such conclusions together, we often reach a third conclusion. This process is deductive reasoning.

(4) We have often heard it said that men of different cultures think differently. Lin Yutang once said that when he thought in Chinese he reached a conclusion different from the one he came to when he thought in English. This does not mean that the process of logical thought is different; it is only that men of different cultures start with different premises. When we say that people of different cultures think differently, we are speaking not of the basic forms of reasoning, but about the values and judgments held in different cultures.

(5) Each culture may have its characteristic ways of presenting ideas in formal public speeches and in formal writing, and if one is writing in a foreign language, he needs to employ expected rhetorical patterns of that language as well as conform to the orthography, the vocabulary, the grammar, and the mechanics of writing in that language.

(6) Let us look at some examples of rhetorical differences across cultures. In English a speaker or writer is expected to state his subject and his purpose as quickly as possible to save the time

of the listener or reader. Japanese modesty may result in an author's beginning by deprecating his ability to write upon the subject when in reality he may be an authority. Japanese readers understand such a procedure as appropriate courtesy. The Navajo Indian, on the other hand, traditionally begins his speeches on any subject by recounting the great deeds of his ancestors and himself, because in his culture one is heeded only if he is considered personally worthy of being heard. In each of these instances, the values of the society are reflected in the rhetorical customs, and the customs make sense to the people who follow them.

(7) Customs in developing a subject differ as well as customs in introductions. In such development, Japanese and Arabic writers, with their tradition of writing for literary purposes, differ markedly from each other and from writers in English. The Japanese have favored elaborating on an idea obliquely rather than forthrightly, so that the author seems to circle an idea. The Arab does quite the opposite. He develops an idea by restating it, making it vivid and giving it impact with piled up metaphors and rich imagery. To both the Japanese and the Arab, learning to express one's ideas in clear and simple language (admired by the English readers) may be a radical change in method. However, clarity and economy of expression are necessary for effective communication in English—especially in formal oral and written discourse.

(8) Above all, this must be remembered: Just as we do not consider that the sounds in one language are better sounds than the sounds in another language or that the grammar in one language is a better grammar than the grammar of another, likewise we make no value judgments about rhetorical patterns. One system of rhetoric is just as good as another and fits the purposes of the culture in which it originated. When we present the rhetorical system of English, all we are saying is that this is the way speakers and writers of English express themselves, and we will try to explain why.

▶ **Exercise 4**

Mark whether each of the following conclusions has been arrived at by deductive (D) or inductive (I) reasoning.

_____ 1. The British do not laugh at the same things that Americans laugh at.

_____ 2. Dr. Brown's final examinations are very long.

_____ 3. Its time to get the furnace in good condition for the winter.

_____ 4. Our neighbors must be away for the weekend.

_____ 5. The food in India is highly spiced.

_____ 6. Tropical species of plants do not thrive in cold climates.

_____ 7. Not all people should go to college.

_____ 8. Debating provides excellent practice in the use of logic.

_____ 9. Men have shorter life expectancy than women.

_____10. Pine trees do not shed their needles in the winter.

▶ Exercise 5

Following are questions for oral discussion.

1. Why is a discussion of ways of thinking fundamental to an understanding of rhetoric?
2. Why did rhetoric refer originally to spoken language?
3. Why can you better understand what a person is trying to say if you know the rhetorical principles of his language?
4. Though rhetorical principles were first analyzed by listening to formal speaking, might these or might they not have originated in informal communication? Give reasons for your answer.

▶ Exercise 6

1. The first paragraph of this essay does not state a thesis sentence. Yet the general subject that the essay is going to discuss is quite clear. What is it?
2. What is the first major point that is being discussed, as indicated in the second paragraph? What topic sentence states this point?
3. The first sentence of paragraph 2 states the first major point about the comparison of rhetorical patterns in different cultures and discusses the first subpoint which supports it. What is this subpoint? The second subpoint is discussed in paragraphs 3 and 4. What is it?
4. What point is being discussed in the fifth paragraph beginning "Each culture may have its characteristic ways . . ."?

5. Name two areas that are discussed in which there are differences in rhetoric in different cultures.
6. The conclusion states the central thesis of the essay. In which sentence did you find it?

Composition

In your courses of study in other classes you will be asked to write answers to examination questions in essay form. These may be based on class lectures and discussions or on material you have read. The following is an examination question you might be asked in a course on composition.

Define rhetoric and tell how a study of it will help you in your writing.

Write your answer. Compare your answer with those of other students.

Choosing a Subject
and Stating It Clearly *How the Author*
and Reader Affect the Choice and the Statement

Write About What You Know and Are Interested In

Before you begin to write on a subject, make sure that you are qualified to discuss it. Pick a subject that reflects your experience, your training, your thinking, and your enthusiasms. Of course you may need to fill in gaps in your knowledge by looking up information in the library or by interviewing someone, but the important thing is that you pick a subject that you know well because of your interest in it and experience with it.

Write About Something That Your Reader Will Be Interested In

Test your subject by asking yourself these questions:

1. Does my subject tell the reader something he does not know?
2. Do I expose an unusual aspect of an old subject?
3. Is the subject inherently interesting to human beings, or will I have to create an interest in it?
4. Is my information up to date and reliable?

Have a Clear Sense of Purpose

Do you want to inform the reader? Do you want him to see what you have seen or feel what you have felt? Do you want him to understand why you hold some belief? Do you want to persuade him to believe as you believe? Of course these purposes are not exclusive of each other. When you inform me about a subject, I may adopt a different attitude toward it, or I may be delightfully entertained while I am being informed. However, a good writer has a primary purpose and a specific one.

Limit Your Subject

It is much better to present a few ideas and develop them well enough for the reader really to understand what you are trying to say than to choose such a broad subject that you only partially describe, or incompletely explain a thing. You can narrow a subject (1) by considering only one aspect or division of it, (2) by limiting it in point of time, or (3) by limiting it in space. In a three-page theme you could not possibly cover the entire field of education, but listed here are some aspects of education that might help you to limit the subject.

Education

Aspect
- of boys, of girls
- of children, adults, the poor, minorities, and so on
- in the basic sciences (or one science), in language (or one language), in art, and so on
- in parochial (religious) schools, public schools, in private schools
- preschool, grade school, high school, college
- in-school curriculum, extracurricular activities
- lunch room, lavatories, classroom, school building, playground, athletic field
- teacher, teacher's aid, school administrator, student, prospective student
- daily classwork, enrichment programs, hourly tests
- for personal growth, for community service, for leisure-time activities, for improving home relationships

	this morning, this week, last month, this year
Time	during my time in the sixth grade
	in this decade, 40 years ago, in the Middle Ages, in 1960
	in (name) School, in (city), in (province, state),
Place	in (country)
	in wealthy neighborhoods, in slums

By combining items from the various categories just given, one might arrive at such limited subjects as these:

The language problems of Mexican-American children on the playgrounds of (*name*) Elementary School in (town), (country), last year

How teacher's aides have helped in supervising the lunch rooms in (school) in (place)

Managing adult education programs in the basic sciences on a limited budget in (school), (place), during the past two years

It is reasonable to expect that such limited subjects can be covered in the space of a student composition.

One final aspect of limiting your subject is that of preserving a point of view. From your interest and experience with the subject, you hold a certain belief about many of the topics you write about. The method or experience or theory you discuss seems to have desirable or undesirable aspects, or both; to have reasons for or against it, or both; or to have advantages or disadvantages, or both. Often part of your writing purpose is to convey to your reader your point of view. Any material that does not contribute to preserving this point of view should be omitted.

PASSAGE FOR STUDY

My Point of View Toward Home[1]

(STUDENT COMPOSITION)

A great many people, when they speak of home, tend to associate it with a certain atmosphere, certain physical surroundings, and certain emotional attitudes within themselves. This sentimentality

---

[1] Mousa El Hafez, Saudi Arabia.

toward home is something that has come down to us from the past. Many modern people do not have it, and I think it is a good thing that they do not.

In the old days life was difficult. Enemies could attack you and kill or rob you, and you had little protection against them. People did not live in well-built houses where doors could be locked. They did not have the protection of an organized police force and telephones which could summon the police instantly. How did this influence the way people felt about home? Small family groups clung tightly together for protection against beasts and against other men. Only the bravest went beyond the small family area. Even in the Middle Ages only the most daring went to lands beyond the sea. The human pursuit of security conditioned men to love their homes, to feel safe only in or near their homes. I am sure that this feeling must have been very strong among the early settlers of the United States who were obliged, by famine and oppression, to take the plunge and go to the new land where they knew no one and where they were subject to Indian attack. We can see this even today in the attitudes of minority groups who, because of a feeling of insecurity, still preserve cohesive family ties.

Today, thanks to modern transportation and well-organized societies, thousands of people willingly and eagerly leave the surroundings where they were born, and the oftener they do so the less sentiment they are likely to have for those surroundings. I lived in England for three years, and I noticed that boys and girls left their parents' homes and lived in dwellings of their own. There you could just pick up the telephone and ask an agency to provide you with a house or an apartment, and that was your home. How has the meaning of this word *home* been altered by such activity? What does home mean to such people or to families who move about living in first one hotel and then another? I believe that for them home means a place where you can have privacy.

This idea of home as being a place of privacy is emerging in my country, Saudi Arabia, where the young are abandoning the parents' homes to live their own kind of life. As for me, the atmosphere and surroundings of the place where my parents live has no sentimental attachment for me. Home is where I can shut the door and be by myself. At the moment it is a room in Eaton Hall. When I left my parents several years ago, I was anxious to leave. You might call it unfeeling, but that is the way I felt. On the day of my departure for the United States, my grandmother sobbed and wept. My father, however, indicated that he understood how I felt.

"Son," he said, "I am not sorry that you are leaving us. I only hope that you make the most of your time."

Bedouins in my country, who are a nomadic people, always living in a changing atmosphere and making their homes where grass and water exist, have a proverb: water pushed by the current does not become stagnant.

▶ **Exercise 1**

1. Does the author of the passage "My Point of View Toward Home" have a point of view that is similar to yours? Explain.
2. Does he discuss his point of view emotionally, or does he present a line of reasoning to support his ideas?
3. Four criteria for choosing a subject are given at the beginning of this lesson; which of the four is (are) best exemplified in this theme? Which least?
4. Is the purpose of this theme to instruct or to persuade? Give the reasons for your answer. Do you think the writer achieved his purpose? Support your point of view.
5. In what way does the conclusion reinforce the central idea of the theme?

▶ **Exercise 2**

The central idea of a piece of writing (1) should be stated specifically (not vaguely) in a thesis sentence, (2) should preferably be a statement, not a question, and (3) should generally predict the organizational pattern of the writing.

Which purpose statement in each of the following pairs would make the best reading if it resulted in a student composition of about a thousand words? Be prepared to defend your choice.

1. a. I am going to tell what a person should see if he visits (my country).
   b. I am going to tell where a person could go to spend an interesting evening in (my country).
2. a. I am going to write about music in my country.
   b. I am going to explain some of the most important reasons why (name of a musician, composer, or singer) is very popular in (country).

3. a. I am going to write about when I was a child.
   b. I am going to show how one early childhood experience has affected the rest of my life.
4. a. I am going to explain how to bargain successfully in countries where bargaining is an expected way to make a purchase.
   b. I am going to explain how trade is carried on in my country.
5, a. I am going to show how the climate of (country) affects the (farm worker).
   b. I am going to explain how the climate of (country) affects life there.
6. a. I am going to write about the attitudes of people in (my country).
   b. I am going to write about certain differences in thinking between (nationality) young people and their parents in regard to _____.
7. a. I am going to write about (Iranian) cooking.
   b. I am going to discuss three important differences between the food of (country) and (a different country).
8. a. I am going to explain the process of hand pollinating date palms in Iran.
   b. I am going to tell about date growing in Iran.

▶ **Exercise 3**

Choose one of the following general subjects and suggest a narrowed aspect of it that you could develop in two pages (about 500 words).

music	family relationships
industry	travel
teachers	games
parents	books
study	work

▶ **Exercise 4**

Make a list of two additional general subjects that you feel qualified to inform someone about. What specific angle of each subject could you treat adequately in a composition of about

500 words? State each in a thesis sentence. Find out from your classmates what thesis they would be most interested in having you develop.

State the Subject Clearly

Make it clear in the introduction

When the television cameramen start with a wide-angle lens and constantly narrow the field of vision until they focus on a very restricted area or a very small detail, they term the process "zooming in." When you write, you often do this in your introduction. You start with background information or related material that eventually focuses attention on the central idea. Then you state this idea clearly. It may be compressed into a single sentence that shows your point of view toward your subject or sets forth the aspect of it that you are going to explain or describe.

Make it clear throughout the composition

Sometimes the central idea is restated or referred to several times during the composition. A convenient time to call the reader's attention to it is when you move from one main point of development of the idea to another. You may use transitional words or phrases such as "The next reason for this condition is . . ." or "Not only . . . but also . . ." or "Then . . ." or "In addition . . ." to refer back to your previous point or your central idea and to introduce what is to come.

Make it clear in the conclusion

In the conclusion you will try to say something that will ensure that the reader cannot possibly forget or misunderstand what you have said. Here are some common ways of ending a composition:

1. A summary.
2. An illustration that reminds the reader of the central idea.
3. A quotation that restates the central idea in a forceful way.
4. A reference to a point made in the introduction. This reference again brings the central idea into focus.

What Home Means to Me[2]

(STUDENT COMPOSITION)

What does home mean to me? Is it the country that I came from? A particular house? The parents by whom I was loved and brought up? The man with whom my happiness is complete? The baby whose birth changed my outlook on life? Home is all the people and all the things that I miss while being away from home.

Jordan, the heir to a rich historical and religious heritage, is my larger home. It extends from the temperate heights of the rugged purple-hued mountains of Moab to the gently rolling hills of Jerusalem; from the deep tropical Jordan Valley, with its luxuriant vegetation, to the Dead Sea, the lowest spot on earth; and from the spectacular sandstone cliffs of Wadi Run to the arid desert of the eastern plateau.

On Jabal Amman, one of the nicest hills in the capital, stands a small red home surrounded by lemon and almond trees with their aroma filling the air. In this little house I started my married life with the man I dearly love. Though simply furnished, the house has all the necessary conveniences and a large collection of souvenirs and wedding presents that we received from our families and friends. The one present I like the most is a sheepskin carpet that I received from my parents. It is made of sixteen lambskins that my family collected from past feasts.

The word *feast* reminds me of feasts at my parents' home where Mother stayed awake a whole night stuffing and cooking a whole lamb for the family to eat when they gathered on a feast day. It reminds me of the children waking up before dawn, waiting impatiently for the morning to approach so that they could exhibit to their friends in the neighborhood their new clothes and shining shoes. Also, I can hear my father's sweet voice in the early morning as he said the morning prayers after the Imam called for them from the minaret.

To me, home is my husband, with whom I have experienced happiness, love, and security. I remember the hot summers when we spent most of the nights out in the garden listening to music or reading because of the intolerable heat inside. I remember our shishkabob parties, where friends would gather around a blazing coal fire eating while more skewers of meat were being broiled.

---

[2] Numati Nurredin, Jordan.

Home reminds me of my husband and me driving to the Dead Sea every month at full moon. The moon reflected its beauty on the sea just as a beautiful woman reflects her beauty in a looking glass.

More than anything else, the word *home* takes me quickly to my dear baby, and I can hear his cry for food and affection. I can feel his little hands scratching my face as he started developing his manual skills. It reminds me of my play time with him when we both rolled over the carpet and his laughter filled the house with joy. It takes me back to the hard time I had to keep him from soaking the kitten with him in the tub as he was taking a bath.

I also remember my neighbors as I say *home*—the easy-going neighbor and the more difficult to please; the quiet, calm neighbor and the vigorous, outspoken one; the shy one and the aggressive one. The neighbor I had the most trouble with lived on the second floor, just above us. She seemed to enjoy clicking over our heads with a noisy pair of slippers that never seemed to wear out.

In a short Arabic poem, two doves from Hijaz decided to migrate to Yemen, and while on their way they stopped on a bush to rest and talk about their trip. A passerby heard them discussing their migration to Yemen and said, "How lucky you are to live there. I wish I could join you."

Before he even finished, one of the doves said to him, "Suppose Eden were not in Yemen; home is still Eden to me."

▶ Exercise 5

1. In the student theme "What Home Means to Me," what is the purpose of the questions in the first paragraph?
2. Where in this theme is the subject (the central idea) stated in a thesis sentence? Is it in an expected place?
3. In what way (ways) does the author zoom in on her subject?
4. In what sentence in each paragraph does the author remind the reader of her subject?
5. In a personal essay such as this one, an author reveals much about himself. What do you learn about this author?
6. Make a list of the types of things you learn about the culture in which the author grew up. Even though this is a very personal expression of feeling, is the essay essentially informative or persuasive? Give the reasons for your answer.
7. How does the conclusion of the theme reinforce the central idea?

Review of Grammatical Patterns: Adjectival Modifiers

In describing her home, the author of "What Home Means to Me" has used various kinds of restrictive modifiers to limit or describe nouns and nonrestrictive modifiers to restate or to give further information.

1. Descriptive or limiting:

Examples

The parents *by whom I was loved and brought up* (relative clause to describe)

The one present *I like the most* (relative clause to limit) (Note omission of the relative pronoun.)

The *temperate* heights of the *rugged, purple-hued* mountains (adjectives to describe)

A *small red* home *surrounded by lemon trees* (adjectives and past participle construction to describe)

2. Giving further information:

Examples

Jordan, *the heir to a rich historical and religious heritage,* (appositive to give further information) (Note use of commas.)

The deep tropical Jordan Valley, *with its luxuriant vegetation,* (prepositional phrase to give further information) (Note use of commas.)

▶ Exercise 6

1. Find three more examples of modifiers used to describe or limit. Indicate what type of modifier is used—adjective, prepositional phrase, relative clause, verbal.
2. Find three more examples of modifiers used to give further information. These will be set off by commas.

Adverbial Modifiers

The author of "What Home Means to Me" has also used modifiers of verbs and of sentences effectively.

Examples

the things that I miss *while being away from home* (subordinator and verbal to indicate time)

It extends *from the temperate heights . . . to the gently rolling hills. . . .* (prepositional phrases to indicate location)

Mother stayed awake *a whole night stuffing and cooking a whole lamb. . . .* (adverbial to show time and participial construction to show purpose)

▶ **Exercise 7**

Find four more different types of adverbials in the selection. Label each type: adverb, prepositional phrase, verbal construction, subordinate clause, absolute construction.[3] Tell what the function of the modifier is—that is, does it tell time, location, manner, or purpose? Does each modify the verb or the sentence?

Composition

Both of the writers of the compositions you have read in this chapter were discussing a subject of personal interest to them, a subject about which they had strong feelings. They made their points of view known in their opening paragraphs.

The author of "My Point of View Toward Home" developed his thesis—that it is a good thing in this modern time not to be sentimental about home—by comparing the past, when the home was a place of refuge, with modern times, when people are constantly moving.

The author of the second essay, "What Home Means to Me," took a similar topic, home, and, like the first author, took a point of view toward it. She illustrated her feeling by giving examples of the things she missed while away from home.

Write a composition on A or B, which follow. Your subject should be something you are deeply interested in or have a strong feeling about. Make your attitude apparent in a topic sentence in the opening paragraph. Develop it throughout by examples.

---

[3] See Lesson 7, Exercise 9, to review absolute constructions (p. 84).

comparisons, or explanations, as in the essays you have just read. Summarize your point of view in a concluding paragraph, or bring that point of view to the attention of the reader again by an apt example or a quotation, as the authors of the student compositions have done.

A. Develop into a two- or three-page composition one of the topics in Exercise 3 or 4 that your classmates liked best.

B. Give your viewpoint toward some aspect of your home, your family, your community or country. Choose something that you have strong personal convictions about. Some topic sentences might be:

1. (Name) is the member of our family who has influenced it most.
2. Our family is made up of a very diverse set of personalities.
3. Things are never dull in our household; a crisis occurs regularly.
4. Each member of our household contributes a great deal to what our family is.
5. Our family history is an interesting one.
6. Many of the things in my family home have sentimental significance for the members.
7. People in my home town follow a boringly routine way of life.
8. I would change certain aspects of life in my hometown if I could.
9. The objections of young people to certain traditional ways of doing things are justified.
10. In traveling, I have discovered ways of doing things which I think should be adopted in my own country.
11. Life is pleasant in (town, country).
12. (Country) affords some of the best scenery in the world.

Developing and Supporting Ideas
Details, Facts, Figures, Examples, Illustration, Quotation

Why Use Supporting Material?

We have seen in the preceding lesson that the reader influences our choice of subject and that he also affects the way in which we introduce our subject to him. He is never closer to us, though, than when we write the body of the composition. He is constantly asking us three questions:

1. How do you know?
2. What do you mean, exactly?
3. Why do you think that?

If we give him satisfying answers to these questions, we will be well on the way to being effective writers.

In this lesson we will consider how we satisfy his demand for answers to the first question, "How do you know?"

If we learn how to answer this question, we find that the same techniques can be used to answer the third question, "Why do you think that?" because explaining a point of view is the basis of persuasion. Ways of answering the second question are discussed in Lesson 13.

We talked earlier about people's constant use of generalizations and assertions—the conclusions we have reached by either inductive or deductive reasoning. If we say "It's a beautiful morning!" our listener is probably beside us seeing the morning, and he can judge for himself the soundness of our statement. But if the reader is not (or has not been) where he can see what we see or hear what we hear, we as writers need to retrace our steps and show the reader what we saw or what we heard or what we read that influenced our thinking.

Does Every Conclusion Need Support?

In reading, we find that such generalizations and assertions are not always the lead-off sentence nor the concluding sentence in a paragraph, but are found sandwiched in between supporting material of various kinds. Not every assertion or generalization is supported; quite often it is not, but if not, the writer has some good reason for omitting the support. Let us study the following paragraph and see how this works.

PASSAGE FOR STUDY

The Charisma of Golden Gate Bridge[1]

Last week I walked across the Golden Gate Bridge from the Marin side toward San Francisco. Now, from a distance, from the Berkeley hills, *this bridge*
Assertion 1 has such a swinging simplicity that it *seems like some natural object:* two great towers rooted in the water, a black horizontal line between them, and looping down from the towers and barely touching the horizontal line, two perfect parabolas of cable. And the whole thing painted a deep chrome red.
Assertion 2 *Bay residents gladly pay exorbitant rents for houses which have a view of the Bridge,* and *few manmade*

[1] Eugene Burdick, "San Francisco: The Metropolis," *Holiday Magazine,* April 1951, 75. Reprinted with permission from *Holiday Magazine* © 1951 The Curtis Publishing Company. Italics added.

Assertion 3	*objects have this power.* From the distance *the Bridge*
Assertion 4	*seems to be not something calibrated, but a powerful tracery, some primitive decoration for the Gate.*

▶ **Exercise 1**

In the preceding selection the author makes four assertions. Only the first is followed by supporting material. Why does he not support his second assertion, that "Bay residents gladly pay exorbitant rents for houses which have a view of the Bridge"? There are two reasons for his not doing this. In preceding paragraphs the author has given so much information about San Francisco that he convinces the reader that he knows the city very well. You are willing to take his word for some things. He does not need to list prices for various kinds of apartments, houses, and hotel accommodations. Such a discussion would divert the reader's mind from the bridge, which is the subject of the paragraph.

Answer these questions about the next two assertions.

1. Why does the author not support Assertion 3?
2. Why does he not support Assertion 4?

How Are Conclusions Supported?

How do we support generalizations and assertions so that our reader will accept them as reasonable? The writer has a wide choice of developmental material. Here are some of the most commonly used kinds.

Specific Details

Giving specific details of what the writer has seen or heard or experienced in some other way is a common method of elaborating a point so that the reader can understand how the writer reached his conclusion. In the following selection, notice how the writer uses specific details to make clear his point that from the Golden Gate Bridge, San Francisco looks orderly and composed, with even the Golden Gate raging quietly.

PASSAGE FOR STUDY

The View from Golden Gate Bridge[2]

Details
(1) As I walked across the Bridge that day, San Francisco looked orderly and composed in the late afternoon light. Seen from above, *the hills flattened out, the skyscrapers around Montgomery and Market were sensible and well-placed, the houses of the Marina bourgeois and orderly, the Embarcadero with its black wharves was a systematic place of commerce.*

Details
(2) To the west the fog bank had moved as it usually does in the late afternoon. During the day it stands offshore like a marble cliff, six hundred miles long, a hundred miles wide and hundreds of feet high. When it moves in close one can see that, *although its edge is razor-sharp, the bank is in a constant, slow, lavalike rolling motion.*

Details
(3) I looked over the edge of the Bridge at the water. The ebb tide had reached a climax, and *the enormous rush of water gave the Gate a humped, quietly raging look. Long lines of flotsam rushed by; bottles, packing cases, a bright orange life jacket. A crab boat came out of the fog bank, and right behind it, moving at three times its speed, a gray destroyer.* Ships move cautiously here, for despite its controlled look this is one of the most dangerous harbor entrances in the world. More than 140 ships have become wrecks in and about the Gate.

▶ **Exercise 2**

Discuss why certain details in the preceding passage are particularly effective.

---

[2] Eugene Burdick, "San Francisco: The Metropolis," *Holiday Magazine*, April 1951, 75. Reprinted with permission from *Holiday Magazine* © 1951 The Curtis Publishing Company. Italics added.

▶ **Exercise 3**

Details are found not only in description. They prove useful in exposition as well. List details in the following passage that the author uses to explain the political difficulties Macedon faced after the death of Philip, the father of Alexander the Great.

The moment life left Philip's scarred body Macedon ceased to be. It was not as if a ship had lost its captain; rather as if a ship, half timbered on the shore, had lost its builder. For Philip, son of Amyntas, had been the brain, the driving force, the general, and the supreme court of the Macedonian clans. No assembly survived him, no experienced ministers existed, to carry on the semblance of a government, nor had Philip named an heir to succeed him. Even his plans for the future remained uncertain, because in his caution he had been at more pains to deceive his enemies than to enlighten his lieutenants.[3]

▶ **Exercise 4**

Suggest specific details which could be mentioned in developing each of the following statements, using the suggestions in number 1 as a guide.

1. He delivered the speech with great skill.

Suggestions:

> The quality of the speaker's voice
> The rate at which he spoke
> His facial expressions
> His air of sincerity
> His rapport with the audience
> His gestures

2. When I stepped out of the door, everything told me it was spring.
3. The room, though expensively furnished, lacked the good taste we would have expected in so famous a man.
4. Even though he was very young, he had the air of someone born to rule.

---

[3] Harold Lamb, *Alexander of Macedon* (Garden City, New York: Doubleday, 1946), p. 64. Copyright 1946, Doubleday and Co., Inc.

5. John takes great pride in his new car.
6. There was something about the man that made me feel I could not trust him.
7. The room looked as though a cyclone had struck it.
8. His opinion of his roommate changed after he had lived with him for several weeks.

Facts

The use of facts is another way to develop an idea. A fact is a statement that can be verified by someone, or that could have been verified by someone in the past, as being the truth. Here are examples of facts:

Our cat has had three litters of kittens.

The Greenwood Hat was written by James Barrie.

There is a new issue of *The Writer's Market* every year.

John Jones was born in Norway.

Facts are indisputable. Because they are indisputable, they are excellent supporting material.

In the preface to an article about Theodore White's newly published book *The Lost Letters of Marie-Louise to Napoleon,* the editors of *Collier's* wrote the following. Note the use of facts to develop the theme.

PASSAGE FOR STUDY

An Intriguing Legacy[4]

The story of how 127 letters of the French empress [Marie Louise] came to lie in the archives of the Swedish royal family is as touched with drama as all things Napoleonic. For it was Désirée who consigned them there.

Fact   *Désirée* was, of course, that famous Frenchwoman who *became Sweden's queen consort* 137 years ago. But much earlier, she had been that delightful and charming Désirée Clary of Marseilles, first love of the youthful Napoleon.

---

[4] Editors of *Collier's,* from the introduction to an article about *The Lost Letters of Marie-Louise to Napoleon* by Theodore White, *Collier's,* August 5, 1955, 63. Italics added.

Fact   *Napoleon's brother,* Joseph, *married Désirée's sister.* But Napoleon wanted for his ambition a woman of nobler stuff than Désirée, daughter of a silk merchant. No woman—not even the superb Josephine, who followed Désirée in Napoleon's life and became his first empress—could satisfy Napoleon's insatiable sense of history until, finally, he married the daughter of the Emperor of Austria, Archduchess Marie-Louise. The letters that we have here are the letters that Marie-Louise wrote him in that climactic year of disaster, 1814. Just before his final exile to Saint Helena, Napoleon gave these precious papers to his brother Joseph, who, in turn, gave them to his sister-in-law Désirée, by then Crown Princess of Sweden and soon to be its queen.

We can only guess at the womanly curiosity with which Désirée, the first love, must have read these letters of Napoleon's last love. After reading them, Désirée apparently ordered the letters packed in a trunk, which eventually was consigned to the palace cellar in Stockholm and forgotten.

▶ **Exercise 5**

Underline other sentences or parts of sentences in "An Intriguing Legacy" that give facts, and report them in class.

▶ **Exercise 6**

Discuss the following questions:

1. What kinds of books, other than biography, are composed mostly of facts?
2. What are the advantages of using facts?
3. Are there any disadvantages in using facts exclusively as a means of development of an idea?
4. What precautions need to be taken when gathering facts?

Figures and Statistics

A. Figures

Figures often make a point perfectly clear. We may say that automobile accidents are increasing, but if we give the number of automobile accidents last year as compared with the number ten years ago, our reader can see the problem much more clearly.

In quoting figures, there are several things that are important to remember:

1. Use only reliable sources for figures.
2. Quote the figures accurately.
3. Make sure the figures are up to date.
4. Present the figures in some kind of rememberable form.

It is easier to remember round numbers than detailed numbers. For example, it is easier to remember "almost two million" than to remember "985,742." And it is easier to remember "over two-thirds" than it is to remember "1,852,968 out of 2,629,479."

In a radio speech several years ago, U.S. Congressman Fred Hartley wanted to show Americans the shocking number of hidden taxes they pay. To be convincing he needed to furnish many figures, but he had the challenge of presenting them in such an interesting manner that people would not get bored and tune to another station. To meet the challenge he did two things. For one thing he pictured the daily routine of a typical American man—getting out of bed, going into the bathroom and turning on the light, using soap and toothpaste, dressing, eating breakfast, driving to work in an automobile, coming home, doing a bit of fishing before dinner, and playing bridge (cards) afterward. For each activity Hartley told what hidden taxes the typical American paid: for sheets, electricity, soaps, dentifrices, clothes (various articles), an automobile, food, etc.

In addition to using narrative to make his material more interesting, Hartley presented the figures in varied forms:

4¢ a pound
3% of the bill
a 5% tax
63 hidden taxes
58 taxes on bread
milk taxed at $1\frac{1}{2}$¢ a quart
medicines taxed at $\frac{1}{3}$ of their cost

In research reports, a reader not only tolerates many figures but expects them, so for the writer the figures do not present a problem. In writing for a general audience, however, a writer needs to plan carefully for effective presentation of many figures.

PASSAGE FOR STUDY

The Wright Brothers' First Airplane Flight[5]

(1) The first Wright Flyer, named for one of their bicycles, was ready by autumn, 1903. A biplane, it had skids like sled runners for undercarriage, flattened wings (a camber of 1 in 20), a wing-span of 40 feet, four inches, a wing area of 510 square feet. It had a biplane elevator in front and a double rudder in the rear. The engine with a chain transmission like a bicycle's, drove two propellers in opposite directions.

(2) Tossing a coin "for the first whack," Wilbur won the privilege of trying the first flight on December 14 at Kill Devil Hills. The Flyer plunged into the sands three and a half seconds after takeoff because of an overcorrection of the elevator, and sustained minor damage that was repaired over the next two days.

(3) On the morning of the 17th, "the conditions were very favorable as we had a cold gusty north wind blowing almost a gale." Under ordinary circumstances they would have waited for safer weather, but they were determined to get home for Christmas dinner with the family and they had faith in their calculations and their skill.

(4) It was Orville's turn. After warming up the engine, he started forward into a 27-mile-an-hour wind. The machine lifted off its wooden-track runway after 40 feet and flew erratically for about 120 feet before darting into the sand. Orville summed up this 12-second flight a decade later: "The first in the history of the world in which a machine carrying a man had lifted itself by its own power into the air in full flight, had sailed forward without reduction of speed, and had finally landed at a point as high as that from which it had started."

(5) The brothers made three other wind-buffeted flights that morning, the last, by Wilbur, covering 852 feet in 59 seconds.

(6) It was noon on December 17, 1903, and two young men with determination, a passion for experiment and scientific method, and an expenditure of less than $1,000, had realized man's most persistent and primordial dream. . . .

---

[5] From the Special Publication, *Those Inventive Americans,* copyright 1971, National Geographic Society, Washington, D.C., pp. 171–172.

(7) Over the next two years the brothers worked to develop the airplane as a practical method of transportation. A friend, Torrence Huffman, let them use a 70-acre pasture between Dayton and Springfield. They made more than 120 flights, mastering banks, turns, circles, figure eights. The press ignored them.

▶ Exercise 7

1. Figures give accurate information about matters such as amount and weight. In the selection you have just read, what other types of information do the figures give?
2. Can you find five words, other than *biplane,* that contain the concept of numbers though figures do not actually appear on the page?
3. In which paragraphs are the most important figures given?
4. Suggest why the author made a separate paragraph of the material in number 5 (i.e., why did he not include this information in paragraph 4?).

B. Statistics

Statistics are figures that are inferred from scientifically selected instances. When polls such as the Gallup poll report that 35 percent of the people of the United States are in favor of a certain governmental policy, their statistics do not indicate that every voter in the United States was queried in order to arrive at that figure. A scientifically determined sample of people from high-income groups, from low-income groups, from middle-income groups, a certain number of Republicans and a certain number of Democrats, and so on, are interviewed. From the figures obtained by interviewing sample numbers of Americans, the pollsters make predictions about the whole group. In order to achieve the accuracy that they do (they estimate that there is between 2 and 3 percent of likely error), the sampling has to be done very scientifically, and the statistics that result have to be used with caution. Used judiciously, statistics provide meaningful information.

In using statistics a writer must make sure of the following:

1. The *source* of the statistics must be a reliable one and must be made known to the reader.

2. The *date* that the statistics were gathered must be relevant to what is being said. If you are writing about current matters, the statistics must be recent.
3. The statistics must be *representative*. They must be scientifically classified. If you write that women are better drivers than men are because women drivers had fewer accidents than men had last year, the reader will want to know whether the fact that women had fewer accidents is the result of there being fewer women who drive cars.

Handle statistics with care.

▶ **Exercise 8**

Advertisers often use statements that sound like statistics, but that have not been scientifically arrived at. For example, a toothpaste advertisement might say, "Four out of every seven people use Superbrite toothpaste." Look through a magazine or a newspaper and find an example in an advertisement of the use of such pseudostatistics. Explain to your classmates why these "statistics" are, in your opinion, not reliable.

Examples

Of all the kinds of developmental material available to the writer, perhaps examples and illustration are used most often. Dwight Eisenhower was noted for his intolerance of subordinates' speaking in generalities. He was constantly saying, "Give me an example." Many of us, like Eisenhower, can see a thing much more clearly when we understand one instance. But we must beware of making a generalization upon the basis of only one instance. One instance does not prove a point. A group of examples is much more effective than one; or an example can be followed by figures that show that the one example is typical.

When Senator Albert W. Hawkes wanted to show his college commencement audience that it is possible for young men to make great achievements, he used examples to prove his point as seen in the following passage.

Success at an Early Age[6]

Alexander Hamilton [first Secretary of the Treasury of the United States] was a lieutenant colonel at 20, a framer of the Constitution of the United States at 30, and Secretary of the Treasury at 32; Alexander Graham Bell invented the telephone at 28; George Eastman produced dry plates for photography at 26; George Westinghouse . . . invented the air-brake at 22; Henry Ford produced his first motor car at 29; Thomas Edison . . . invented the incandescent lamp at 32; the Wright brothers were 32 and 36, respectively, at the time of their first air flight; Woolworth established his first store when he was 24; John D. Rockefeller organized the Standard Oil Company when 31. . . .

This is the "march of youth" instead of the "march of time," and it indicates what is expected of you in the crisis ahead.

▶ **Exercise 9**

A. The examples in the selection you have just read support the contention that it is possible for young men to make great achievements at an early age. List at least three examples that you might use to support one of the following generalizations:

1. Sons of famous men rarely achieve the greatness of their fathers.
2. A number of theories have been advanced as to how man first came to the American continents.
3. The climate in which people live affects the kind of food they eat.
4. Many scientific discoveries have been made as the result of keen observation.

Compare your examples with those given by your classmates.

B. Write three generalizations or assertions that might be supported with examples. Discuss in class what examples might be used to support them.

---

[6] Albert W. Hawkes, "Individual Responsibility and Freedom," *Vital Speeches,* August 1, 1946, 632–633.

Illustration

Illustration is an extended example. Of all forms of support, illustration is one of the most popular. Since they stimulate his imagination, and often contain human interest, illustrations hold the attention of your reader. Illustrations are most effective when the writer's point is supported by other material as well as by illustration. One example or one illustration by itself might be atypical. But if by furnishing facts or figures or quotations from an authority you can show that it is typical, illustration is a forceful means of making a point clear and convincing. The following passages uses illustration to show the miracle of animal instinct.

PASSAGE FOR STUDY

Animal Wisdom

Man can only marvel at the miracle of instinct—at how various animals and insects, in order to perpetuate their species, unerringly complete a complicated process which no one taught them.

Take the case of the mud dauber wasp, so common in the barns and attics in the United States. The mother constructs a mud nest composed of hundreds of tiny mud cells. After she fashions each cell, she stings a spider (not killing it, only anaesthetizing it), puts it in the cell, and lays an egg upon it. Then she seals the cell with mud and begins to construct another cell, repeating the process of providing food for her newborn and then laying the egg. The mother dies before the young are hatched, but the young wasp has been provided with vital fresh food enough to last him until he can forage for himself. When the new female wasp gets to be an adult, she too will know, without being shown, exactly how to do this.

Some species are forced by instinct to make long journeys in order to mate and reproduce in an optimum environment for the young. Toward the end of summer the female eel, whether eastern American or western European, heads for the Sargasso Sea south of Bermuda. Females who have lived in rivers and fresh water lakes inland swim to the Atlantic ocean. When they near it, they are joined by males who have lived in the brackish water near the mouths of rivers; together they make the long trek south. At three thousand feet down the females lay millions of eggs, the males fertilize the eggs, then the grown eels die. The youth hatch within days, spend a year going back to the United States, three years to Europe. The females return to the same pools their mothers came from and live there from four to eight years until instinct demands that they go to the Sargasso Sea again and spawn and die.

The Chinook salmon is another famous migrator for spawning. Unlike the eel, the salmon spends a large part of its life in the ocean and ascends the rivers to spawn in fresh water, sometimes traveling as many as a thousand miles to mate and lay its eggs in the exact locale where it itself was hatched. The salmon enters the river in early spring, going up in leisurely fashion, but overcoming the difficulties of any barrier—such as water falls—which they encounter. If the water is too warm when they arrive, they wait until it is 54 degrees or lower. The male fights with other males, the winner mates with the females. The female digs her nest in the gravel bed, lays her eggs, covers them, and departs. The parents promptly die. The young, when hatched, do not remain in the river but swim to the sea. However, when its life is nearly over, any salmon makes the supreme effort to return to its birthplace to spawn before it dies. Such creatures had to do all these things right the first time or else their species would have gone the way of the mastadon. Man has yet to solve the mystery of how they know.

▶ **Exercise 10**

Rewrite this selection in two or three sentences using examples instead of illustrations to support the topic sentence. In other words, condense the information given about the wasp, the eels, and the salmon, until each constitutes an example rather than an illustration.

Why are these examples less convincing than the illustrations?

Why are these examples that you have just written not convincing, whereas the examples in "Success at an Early Age" were convincing?

▶ **Exercise 11**

The following story might well be used to illustrate a point about writing. Read the illustration, and then write a concluding paragraph in which you relate the illustration to advice you would give to a beginning writer. Then give the entire selection a title.

Each person puts the stamp of his personality upon what he does. David Ewen illustrates this point in a story he tells about Fritz Kreisler, the violinist. Once in Amsterdam, as he passed a pawn shop where cheap violins were displayed in the window, Kreisler gave way to an impulse to enter the shop and ask the pawnbroker how much he would give Kreisler for his own violin—of course an expensive instrument. The pawnbroker looked at the violin carefully and abruptly left the shop only to return shortly with a policeman. He told the officer to arrest Kreisler—that here was a man who had obviously stolen one of Kreisler's violins. Kreisler protested that he was indeed himself, but he did not have his passport with him to prove it. Finally he grabbed the violin and began to play it.

"He's right," the pawnbroker said. "He *is* Fritz Kreisler. Nobody else could play *that* way."[7]

Quotation from Authority

In order to support a point we sometimes need to quote someone else who is an authority on the subject and whose judgment our readers will respect. When we do this we must make sure that the one we quote is really an authority and that our readers will recognize him as such. If they may not know him we can give some information to indicate his competence.

Here is an example of use of quotation from authority:

Every day Americans will appear at American consulates all over the world to report the loss of their passport and wallet. They need money. Certainly the consulate must have emergency funds for stranded Americans? It hasn't. To be exact, the consul has some very limited funds for "extremely restricted circumstances," but the loss of a tourist's wallet is not one of them. . . .

"We cannot lend tourists money, we cannot cash or endorse personal checks, we are not permitted to make private loans," a consul

---

[7] Adapted from David Ewen, *Listen to the Mocking Words* (New York: Arco, 1945), p. 42.

says. "We are not bankers. We assist them in getting money from home. We call their relatives or banks, collect. . . ."[8]

Sometimes we quote the words of someone else, not just because he is an authority on the subject, but because he has phrased the idea better than we could possibly do it ourselves. Wendell Phillips, a great American orator before and during the Civil War, used such a quotation when he was trying to show the difference between a monarchy and a republic.

Accept proudly the analysis of Fisher Ames: "A monarchy is a man-of-war, staunch, iron-ribbed, and resistless when under full sail; yet a single rock sends her to the bottom. Our republic is a raft, hard to steer and your feet always wet, but nothing can sink her."

▶ **Exercise 12**

Discuss with your classmates possible forms of support that would be appropriate for two of the following topic sentences for a composition. Before the discussion, prepare notes similar to those following the first topic sentence. For this exercise use as many actual facts, figures, and so on, as you have at your command without having to go to the library. However, if you can think of certain types of supporting material that you do not have but that you could reasonably expect to obtain through research, include those too. After your notes are collected, you may want to modify your topic sentence.

1. Television has had a great effect upon today's children. (Consider the positive effects as well as the negative.)

   Facts:

   Sesame Street and *Misterogers* have had high ratings as educational programs for three years.

   The *National Geographic* films and *The Wild Kingdom* acquaint children with faraway places and the wildlife of the world.

---

[8] Joseph Wechsberg, "U.S. Consuls: Trouble Is Their Business," *Holiday Magazine,* April/May 1974, 31–32. Reprinted with permission from *Holiday Magazine* © 1974 The Curtis Publishing Company.

Figures:

It is estimated that many children spend as many as five hours a day in front of the TV screen.

Fifty percent of the programs on TV show violence of some sort.

Testimony:

(Name), a Detroit psychiatrist, says that TV violence has little effect on a child.

However, our neighbor, Mrs. (name), says that Johnny couldn't sleep last night after having watched *Monster Feature.*

Illustration:

Last night's newspaper reported a tragedy in which a small boy had killed another while they were playing that they were cowboys and cattle rustlers.

However, *Upstairs-Downstairs* is a wonderful illustration of a play that re-creates a historical period (in this case, Edwardian England).

2. A person gets most of his education outside the classroom.
3. The traditional dress of the (nationality) is quite different from the traditional dress of the (nationality).
4. The traveler learns the hard way about differences in currency among nations.
5. A man need not be old in order to accomplish significant things.
6. Taxes in (country) are too high.
7. To be a champion tennis player one must have certain personal qualifications as well as knowledge of the game.
8. The best things in life are (are not) free.

Grammar Review

A. A further look at modification

The details that develop an idea may be presented as complete sentences or in some instances as reductions of sentences. Compare the two selections that follow and judge which form makes the details more vivid in a description. Tell why.

1. *Details Presented in Complete Sentences*
   This bridge . . . seems like some natural object. Its two great towers are rooted in the water. There is a black horizontal line between them. Two perfect parabolas of cable loop down from the towers and touch the horizontal line. The whole thing is painted a deep chrome red.
2. *Details Presented in Reductions of Sentences*
   This bridge seems like some natural object: two great towers rooted in the water, a black horizontal line between them, and looping down from the towers and barely touching the horizontal line, two perfect parabolas of cable. And the whole thing painted a deep chrome red.

► **Exercise 13**

A. Combine the following sentences into one sentence containing appropriate structures of modification. Use the sentence describing the Golden Gate Bridge as a model.

The desert appeared like the surface of the moon. It stretched endlessly before me. It was marked with slight ripples like some ocean floor. A few boulders rose up here and there. They were covered with powdery flakes. The whole scene was devoid of any color save a yellowish grey.

B. In "The View from the Golden Gate Bridge" find verbal constructions that modify nouns. Would you expect to find them in passages that are primarily narrative, expository, or descriptive?

B. Verb forms

► **Exercise 14**

Note the verb forms that are used in the example passages in this lesson, and answer the questions that follow.

1. In the passage "The View from the Golden Gate Bridge," a variety of tenses and verb forms are used.

   { To the west the fog bank *had moved* . . .
   { During the day it *stands* . . .

$$\left\{ \begin{array}{l} \text{I } \textit{looked} \text{ over the edge of the Bridge . . .} \\ \text{The ebb tide } \textit{had reached} \text{ a climax . . .} \end{array} \right.$$

Explain why each of these verb forms is used.
2. Why is the present tense used in "Animal Wisdom"?

Composition

Take one of the topic sentences in Exercise 13 as your subject for a composition of about 500 words. Use at least three different types of support to develop the topic. Indicate the types of support in the margin of your paper.

Organizing the Composition
Time Order, Space Order, Topical Order

Patterning Ideas

Present your ideas as organized regiments of soldiers—in marching order. This will help to make your writing instantly apparent.

In the preceding lesson we discussed how to develop a single assertion with supporting material (facts, figures, examples, etc.). Sometimes such activity is called a single-cell composition. The selection "Language and Culture" in Lesson 7 is an example. Answers in an essay examination are also often single-cell writing. But most of our writing is more complex and requires knowledge of how to arrange a series of assertions, each of which works with the others to support a thesis sentence, which states the central idea. The major assertions we have referred to as main points. *These main points should be clearly stated in a composition and should clearly relate to the thesis sentence and to each other.*

Patterns of Arrangement
of Expository Material

1. Time (chronological) order

In *Evenings with Music* Syd Skolsky devotes one chapter to a thumbnail history of music. The thesis sentence is as follows:

The music that we know today, the musical instruments with which we have become familiar, the forms that we have studied—all have been the subject of slow evolution.

Beginnings of successive paragraphs are as follows:

Before he was able to speak, *prehistoric man* . . .

At the beginning of *the seventh century* . . .

Then *about the year 1000* . . .

The story of music *for the next four centuries* . . .

With the discovery *in the fifteenth century* of the East and its rich treasures, and with the opening up of commerce and trade . . .

Toward the *middle of the 1720's* . . .

The death of Bach (*1750*) and Händel (*1759*) brought the polyphonic period to a close . . .

The material about music in this chapter has obviously been arranged in a time sequence. Time order is used in stories, to show the development of a science or to mark the steps of a process, and it is widely used in history books. It may be used to organize material in a paragraph or a longer piece of writing.

▶ **Exercise 1**

1. What words in the thesis sentence of Skolsky's chapter reveal the form of arrangement that the chapter will follow.
2. Is the time lapse the same between each of the periods of music that are mentioned? Why did the author not give an account of the state of music every 100 or 200 years (i.e., at perfectly regular intervals)?

▶ **Exercise 2**

Choose a subject—a game, a sport, a profession such as medicine, a vocation such as some form of agriculture, or the state of some academic discipline such as chemistry or the learning of foreign languages. Indicate what periods of time reflect changes that are important. Fill in the blanks that follow to show a time pattern of organization that you might use in writing a composition on the subject.

Thesis sentence: _____

_____

Beginnings of successive paragraphs (or other successive portions of the composition):

_____

_____

_____

_____

_____

2. Space order

It may be convenient to arrange material from north to south, bottom to top, inside to outside, far to near, or some other spatial sequence that is easy for the reader to follow. Such spatial arrangement may be used in a paragraph, in a longer section of a composition (such as the introduction), or as the form of arrangement for an entire chapter or composition.

PASSAGE FOR STUDY

The Antarctic: Home of the Wind[1]

Now that we have followed the story of its [Antarctica's] discovery in detail, it is time that we had a look at the continent as a whole.

If we began with its appearance as seen from the moon by the first human to reach it, the Antarctic would remind him strongly of what the astronomers see when they look at the planet Mars. A more or less round patch of dead white would surround the Pole itself, and it would wax and wane as winter passed into summer, though not so markedly as on Mars.

If an observer contented himself with a space ship only a few thousand miles above the earth's atmosphere, he would make out more interesting details. . . . A closer view would show that calm and silence are the very last adjectives to apply to the Antarctic,

---

[1] Frank Debenham, *Antarctica* (New York: Macmillan and London: Herbert Jenkins, Ltd., 1961), pp. 124–126. © Frank Debenham 1959. Used by permission.

for it is the Home of the Wind. If our observer from above could see the wind . . . he would see a continent covered with a moving sheet of air flowing always to the left as is the way with winds in the Southern Hemisphere.

If he were hovering only a few hundred feet up . . . he would see, on three days out of every four, the loose snow being driven over the firm snow, a spindrift of tiny particles veiling the furrows caused by the wind and building long streamers of hard snow behind every obstacle, pointing outwards towards the edge of the continent. The details of this wind-sculptured surface could be seen through a thin drift in a light wind, but as the wind grew stronger the layer of whirling snow would get thicker till in a full blizzard it would be 100 feet thick and so dense that visibility would be reduced to a single meter's distance.

▶ **Exercise 3**

1. What spatial pattern is used in the selection about Antarctica? What words indicate this pattern?
2. Does this selection constitute an entire composition, or is it a part of a longer piece of writing? What sentence gives you a clue? Comment on the function of paragraph 1.

▶ **Exercise 4**

Using the pattern that follows, make an outline for a composition describing how some historical figure acquired power through acquisition of territory. Use spatial order rather than time order for the account. How does space arrangement of main points affect the phrasing of the thesis sentence?

Thesis sentence:
   I.
   II.
   III.

▶ **Exercise 5**

The paragraphs about Antarctica zoom in on the subject. That is, they narrow the focus from a wide area to a smaller one as the motion picture cameraman does when he wants to focus more closely on something. Using this pattern of arrangement, describe some person you know well. What would you notice about him from a distance (such as across a soccer field), from a middle distance (such as across a room), then close up (such as sitting across a table from him in a restaurant)?

Phrase some unifying central idea for your thesis sentence. Perhaps the faraway impression of the person was not a correct one. Perhaps the close-up view verifies your first opinion.

Remember that the best description contains details gained through other senses as well as through sight.

3. Topical order

When a writer uses topical order he divides his subject into parts according to some principle of classification or logical division of ideas, and then discusses the parts one by one. Some common methods of classification are:

1. Classification or division on the basis of fields of inquiry:
   a. physical
   b. mental
   c. religious
   d. social
   e. economic
   f. political
2. Classification as to kinds of cause or kinds of effect:
   a. primary cause
   b. contributing cause
   c. precipitating cause
   d. immediate effects
   e. long-range effects
3. Classification on the basis of physical characteristics:
   a. color
   b. size
   c. atomic weight
   d. reaction to other elements
   e. boiling point

These forms of classification just listed are only a few that might be mentioned. Topical order is by far the most common arrangement of ideas in English.

The Influence of the American Indian on American Culture[2]

When European explorers reached the coasts of North, South, and Central America in the fifteenth and sixteenth centuries, they found these areas inhabited by numerous tribes—tribes that differed greatly in government, religion, social customs, and temperament. A few of the civilizations in Central and South America had reached great heights. For instance, the Mayas had perfected a calendar one ten-thousandth of a day more accurate than the one we use today, with an error of less than five minutes a year. Although their literature has been lost, an observer in the 1560's reported that the Mayas had written in many intellectual areas: astrology, prophecy, theology, legend. The Inca culture in Peru and the Toltec and Aztec cultures in Mexico were also very highly developed. These people were great builders, great traders, skilled farmers, and artisans in metal and cloth.

While these cultures in Central and South America were particularly outstanding, characteristic civilizations had developed among the Indians of North America as well. As the people from Europe settled the western continents, some of their customs filtered into the way of life of the Indian people, but there was a cultural exchange and the Indian cultures influenced the Europeans too.

In North America, Indian culture seeped into American life in innumerable ways. Indian names were given to cities and regions, thus preserving the memory of famous tribes and chieftains. The states of Delaware, Iowa, Illinois and Alabama were named after Indian tribes. The Monongahela and the Susquehanna, the Arickaree, the Seneca and the Mohawk Rivers have Indian names; so do the cities of Spokane, Yakima, Walla Walla, Cheyenne, Omaha, Wichita, Natchez, Miami, Biloxi, Mobile, Chicago. The Mojave Desert, the Ute Pass through the Rocky Mountains, Narragansett Bay, Lake Cayuga, Lake Huron, and Lake Erie—these too are Indian names. In Colorado the Arapahoe Indians left many place names. A street in Denver, a street in the nearby city of Boulder, a county, a glacier, a ski area, twin mountain peaks—all are named Arapahoe. In other sections of the country a similar Indian influence is apparent. It is reflected not only in place names, but also

---

[2] Details about the Mayan culture and the federation of the League of the Iroquois were obtained from William Brandon, *The American Heritage Book of Indians* (New York: Dell, 1961).

in the names of many commercial enterprises. A few examples are: Mohawk rugs, the Mohawk Airline, the Pontiac automobile, the Erie Railroad, Pequot household linens, and Oneida silver products.

Every American owes a particular debt to the Iroquois Indians. Living in what is now New York state, the Iroquois were perhaps the most sophisticated politically of all the Indian tribes in North America. Several nations of one branch of the Iroquois (called the "Five Nations") were joined in a confederacy called the "League of the Iroquois." According to the Indian legend, a wise and good statesman, Deganawidah, had organized the League to put an end to the quarreling and warring among the Five Nations and establish a government based upon law. Under the League each of the Five Nations remained sovereign in its own domestic affairs, but acted as a unit in matters that concerned relations with other Indian nations. The confederacy kept the tribes of the Five Nations from fighting each other, and the federation proved valuable in diplomatic relations with other tribes. When a chief said, "I speak for all the Five Nations," the opinion was not to be regarded lightly. While in actual practice all did not run smoothly within the League, the League was certainly a fact in the minds of the leaders. Each summer the great council of the League was held at the most important town of the Onondaga tribe. This was an impressive occasion and kept the Iroquois alive to the reality of the federation. When the thirteen English colonies in America were considering what kind of government to establish after they had won their independence from England in the latter part of the eighteenth century, Benjamin Franklin suggested that they establish a confederacy similar to that of the Iroquois. The convention agreed, and the government of the United States under the Articles of Confederation was influenced by the federated government of the Five Nations of the Iroquois.

Art is another field in which the United States has been influenced by Indian culture. Indian jewelry in silver and turquoise is featured in many stores. Because it is popular, non-Indian Americans copy the styles; but genuine Indian jewelry commands respect. Beaded leather-work, as that on shoes and belts, is also popular, and Indian weaving (in rugs particularly) is admired. Many American homes in the southwestern United States make extensive use of Indian rugs. In other parts of the country it is not unusual to see a house furnished with many items of Indian origin: with pictures, rugs, cochinas (carved wooden representations of Indian gods), the lovely black pottery of the San Ildefonso and the Santa

Clara tribes, or the uniquely decorated pottery of the Acoma or Hopi tribes. Indian dances, too, engage the interest of Americans of all racial and national backgrounds. People travel for hundreds of miles to see the ceremonial dances in such cities as Gallup, New Mexico, or Flagstaff, Arizona, and the dances at the pueblos near Santa Fe and Taos, New Mexico. Often Boy Scout groups study these dances carefully and learn them, paying careful attention to make the details of their performance authentic.

Perhaps the way in which Indian culture has most greatly affected the everyday life of the United States is in the eating habits of the people. The Indian tribes in North, Central, and South America were generally skilled farmers. They knew about fertilization, irrigation, and seed selection. Three-fifths of all the varieties of agricultural products found around the world were known to them, and they introduced many new products to the people of Europe: the white and the sweet potato, maize, manioc (from which tapioca is made), cacao (chocolate), rubber, vanilla, peanuts, avocados are but a few. Stories are told about how the Indians taught the early English settlers their methods of fertilizing the ground. Potatoes and maize particularly have become staples in the diet of the modern American, and the raising of maize—Americans now call it "corn"—has greatly contributed to the wealth of leading agricultural states in the country. The American Indian also introduced tobacco to the early European settlers. Tobacco was the crop that brought wealth to the early colonies; it remains one of the leading products of the country today.

Concerned as he was with America's past and America's future, John F. Kennedy advocated making the study of Indian history a requisite for all young Americans. Perhaps he sensed that for a relatively new country, many of whose citizens have been recently transplanted from other continents, the Indian's greatest contribution lies in the feeling of permanence, the sense of continuance, which their history furnishes the nation. People in the United States are indeed indebted to the American Indian for what his race has contributed and is continuing to contribute to the culture of the nation.

▶ **Exercise 6**

Answer the following questions on the selection you have just read.

1. Fill the spaces that follow with a suitable statement of each of the main points in the article on the Indian influence on American culture. You may be able to use the exact wording in the article or may need to modify it somewhat. Compare your list of main points with those of your classmates.

Thesis sentence: In the United States, five important aspects of the culture of the Indians have seeped into the daily life of modern-day Americans.

I. _____

II. _____

III. _____

IV. _____

V. _____

2. Identify the pattern of organization of "The Influence of the American Indian on American Culture."

3. In view of the thesis sentence (central idea) of this selection, can you justify the discussion of South and Central American Indian cultures? In what sentence do the authors attempt to justify it?

4. How does the type of content of the last paragraph in this article differ from that in most concluding paragraphs?

Selecting and Arranging Main Points

Here are some of the principles of selecting and arranging main points in a longer composition.

1. *Use one consistent pattern of arrangement.* For example, if you start with topical order, do not switch midway to time order or some other pattern. If you do so, your reader may become confused.

2. *Limit the number of main points to what you can develop ade-*

quately in the amount of time you have and the amount of space allowed.

3. *Divide the material so that the main points do not overlap.* No two points should discuss the same idea.
4. *Do not leave out any essential part.*

▶ **Exercise 7**

1. Examine the following brief outlines and tell which you consider the best.
2. What is wrong with each outline you reject? Use the principles that you have just studied as a basis for your judgment. Compare your answers with those of your classmates.

Mini-Outline I

Thesis sentence: Airplanes are useful in doing the work on a ranch.

  I. Ranchers use planes for checking the water supply for the stock.

  II. Ranchers use planes to locate breaks in fences.

  III. Ranchers use planes to get new parts for broken machinery.

  IV. Ranchers find planes a great help in the summer.

  V. Ranchers find planes a great help in the fall.

Mini-Outline II

Thesis sentence: The education of a doctor continues after his graduation from medical school.

  I. As an intern, he studies diagnostic procedures.

  II. The American Medical Association reports that a practicing physician spends at least two hours a day studying medical journals.

  III. As a resident physician he takes part in the experimental work done at the hospital.

  IV. As a practicing physician he reads articles in the medical journals that report new medicines, treatments, and surgical procedures.

Mini-Outline III

Thesis sentence: George Washington Carver always tried to create something useful from waste materials.

I. He salvaged useless parts of plants to create new products.

II. Through his teaching he salvaged what might have been wasted human lives (of his black students).

III. He salvaged his own life from its lowly beginnings and became an influential public figure.

Outlining: Forms and Uses

Experienced writers find an outline an easy way of checking the organization of their ideas before they start writing.

In an essay examination your outline may be a list of topics you should cover in your answer. For example, if the essay question were "Discuss the ways in which American faith in education was demonstrated anew after World War II," you might jot down these topics:

G.I. bill
consolidation
Fed. Aid
Roman Catholic schools
adult educ.

Such an outline is meaningful to the writer, but it may not be meaningful to someone who does not know what your abbreviations stand for or what ideas your words indicate.

Most useful for purposes of your composition class is the outline in which you state your thesis sentence and the main points in complete sentences, and in which you indicate the kinds of support you will furnish for each main point. Here is a master plan for outlining. Following it is an example of how a student's outline can grow out of the master plan. Note that the supporting material is indicated in brief fashion to save the student and the instructor time.

Master Plan
for an Outline

Specific purpose. Before beginning to write your outline, state what you expect to accomplish—to explain, describe, define, or whatever—keeping your reader and your time and space limitations clearly in mind. Label your aim as: *Specific Purpose.* As you write, check each idea, illustration, and supporting statement to be sure that it clearly relates to your purpose. Your thesis sentence grows out of your purpose. If the thesis sentence is already stated, you do not need a separate statement of purpose in your paper. The stating of the purpose in the outline is to guide your thinking in planning the paper.

Thesis sentence. State in a complete sentence your specific point of view or the specific aspect of the subject you plan to explain or support. Label this as *Thesis Sentence.*

I. *Main division of material* (or *supporting statement*)
  (This must be a sentence.)
  A. *Subordinate division of material*
     (This must be a sentence.)
     1. *Developmental or supportive material to be used*
        (Can be stated in short sentences or phrases. Each item should clearly relate to the subpoint, which clearly relates to the main point, which, in turn, clearly relates to the thesis sentence. You may wish to identify in the margin the type of developmental material you use.)
     2. ⎫
     3. ⎬ *Additional developmental material*
  B. *Second subordinate division of material*
     (This must be a sentence.)
II. *Main division of material* (or *supporting statement*)
  A. *Subordinate division of material*
     1. ⎫
     2. ⎬ *Developmental material*
  B. *Second subordinate division of material*

Sample Student Outline[3]

Specific purpose: To show that people's attitudes toward home have changed for very good reasons.

Thesis sentence: It is good that the ancient sentimentality toward home is not preserved by everyone today.

	I. In ancient times home meant security.
Development:	No well built houses, telephones, police
Details and	protection. So the family group consti-
Reasoning	tuted the protection.
	II. Today home means a place where you can have privacy.
Example	Young people leaving home early (in England)
Example	My present home: Eaton Hall
Quotation	Quotation from my father

When you write the composition from an outline such as the preceding one, you will want to add an introduction and a conclusion as well as transitional phrases or sentences to relate the main points to the thesis sentence and to each other. The outline is useful, however, in showing the framework of your thinking.

For another type of subject, a quite different type of outline best serves the purpose. Some subjects require explanation which is not easily made apparent by jotting down words or phrases. In such a case, a sentence outline is most useful. All items in such an outline are sentences.

Sample Sentence Outline

Specific purpose: To explain how people breathe.

Thesis sentence: Breathing is based upon changes of air pressure within the thorax.

I. Inhalation involves air rushing into a cavity in which air pressure has been lowered.

---

[3] This is an outline of the student theme on pp. 115–116 of Lesson 10.

A. The thoracic cavity is enlarged by unconscious processes directed by the medulla.
   1. The intercostal muscles lift the ribcage and move it outward to form a larger cavity.
   2. The diaphragm is flattened, also producing a larger cavity.
B. As the thoracic cavity is enlarged, the air pressure within the lungs is decreased.
C. To fill the partial vacuum in the lungs and equalize the air pressure inside and outside the body, atmospheric pressure forces air into the lungs.

II. Exhalation involves air rushing out of a cavity in which air pressure has become greater than air pressure outside the body.
A. Pressure is built up in several ways.
   1. The intercostal muscles relax and allow the ribcage to fall and to decrease the size of the thoracic cavity.
   2. The diaphragm relaxes and returns to its dome shape; also decreasing the size of the cavity.
B. When the air pressure becomes greater within the lungs than outside, the pressure is released, and exhalation takes place.

Questions Students Ask About Outlining

1. Must there always be at least two main points (or two subpoints) in an outline?

Answer: It depends upon what type of material you are outlining. If you are dealing with exposition, in which you are sorting ideas, there must always be at least two points. If you see only one subpoint, you should incorporate the idea into your main point.

If, however, you are arguing a point, you may have only one good reason for believing as you do, and one good reason is sufficient. Thus only one reason appears in the outline.

2. In an outline must I always have a thesis sentence, or can I just list my developmental or supportive material?

Answer: Your thesis sentence is the most important single item in your planning. Unless you have one, you are likely to stray from the subject. Furthermore, all of your developmental material stems from your thesis, or central idea. It controls everything that follows.

3. Does outlining always have to precede the writing of a composition? Doesn't it inhibit me in what I want to say?

Answer: All writers agree that an outline is a check on your basic thinking. Some writers find it useful to outline first. Other writers who are willing to rewrite often wait until a composition is written and then outline the material. This latter group are often writers of material in which style is highly important. For practical writing, such as the writing in school, in which the ideas that are presented are more important than the kind of phrasing used, it is better to outline first so that the basic development of thought is clear and adequate in the initial draft.

▶ **Exercise 8**

Which of the three patterns of organization discussed in this lesson (time, space, topic) might best be used to develop each of the following thesis sentences?

1. A student's life becomes more complicated as each term progresses.
2. A student has many reasons for attending a university.
3. Many students find satisfaction in activities other than their studies.
4. The lectures of Professor Smith are extremely interesting.
5. Traveling across my country is a liberal education.
6. Planning a border of flowers requires careful thought.

▶ **Exercise 9**

Determine what aspects of the following outline are wrong. Be especially critical of the selection of main points. Refer to the principles of selecting and arranging main points which you studied earlier in this lesson, pp. 152–153. Rewrite the outline, making changes in the form and the wording that seem desirable. Be prepared to give reasons for the changes you make.

Thesis sentence: The saying "Two can live as cheaply as one" is not true.

   I. A young couple should not marry under the illusion that two can live as cheaply as one.
  II. The important reasons why a young couple cannot live as cheaply as one.
     A. The couple needs food enough for both.
     B. The couple needs clothes enough for both.
     C. Household items cost more for two people than for one.
     D. Enjoyable married life includes recreation.
     E. Transportation will be involved in married life.
 III. For a prosperous marriage young couples should not be tempted by sayings like "Two can live as cheaply as one."

▶ **Exercise 10**

Transitional sentences or phrases help the reader to follow your thought from one point to another. The sentences that follow are taken from James Harvey Robinson's *Mind in the Making.*[4] They state main points and transitions between main points. Prepare an outline of this material on the basis of the information given you here. If any necessary element in the outline is missing, phrase it yourself. Between the main points in your outline, insert transitional material as appropriate and label it "Transition."

A third kind of thinking is stimulated when anyone questions our beliefs and opinions. . . . Most of our so-called reasoning consists in finding arguments for going on believing as we already do.

---

[4] James Harvey Robinson, *Mind in the Making* (New York: Harper & Row, 1921), pp. 46, 39, 48, 39 respectively.

The reverie . . . is frequently broken or interrupted by the necessity of a second kind of thinking. We have to make practical decisions.

This brings us to another kind of thought which can fairly easily be distinguished from the three kinds above . . . it is that peculiar species of thought [i.e., creative thought] which leads us to change our mind.

When uninterrupted by some practical issue we are engaged in what is now known as the reverie.

Composition

Write on one of the following:

A. Earlier in this chapter you studied an outline that explained the process of breathing. Describe some process in your field of study which would be of interest to your classmates. To help you arrange the steps of the process in an orderly form, prepare an outline before you start to write. Turn in the outline for instructor approval before you write the paper.

B. In a three-page composition, tell how to do one of the following:

1. care for some piece of equipment (gun, tennis racket, skis, a boat, a car)
2. care for some piece of furniture (article of clothing)
3. apply for a job
4. prepare for an examination
5. make friends in a strange town
6. choose a vocation
7. be a good ambassador for your country when you travel
8. get the most out of a vacation
9. win at some game or sport
10. write an interesting letter to friends or relatives
11. bargain successfully in a market in (country)
12. adjust to living conditions in a foreign country
13. recognize an excellent horse (precious stone, restaurant, melon, crafted item, fruit or vegetable)

Outline your material before you start writing; turn in the outline for instructor approval before you write the paper.

C. Describe a change in your country in a field like public health, the status of women, education, or language. In the introductory paragraph state what the condition is. Then in succeeding paragraphs, trace the change as it developed. Refer to the thesis sentence from time to time and relate your main points to it. Outline your material before you start to write. Turn in your outline for instructor approval before writing the paper.

Making Ideas Clear *Definition,*
Comparison, Contrast, Explanation, Restatement

Each writer must anticipate when his reader will ask: What do you mean? It is at that point that the writer must define his terms, perhaps compare or contrast what he has been writing about with something the reader might already know, explain in more detail, or restate his idea in other words. This lesson is concerned with these methods of making ideas clear.

Definition

Two types of words need defining: (1) technical words (for example, *magnetic field, necrology, morpheme*) and (2) words that are used so frequently that they lose all their specific meanings (for example, *good, education, justice, power, wrong, democracy*).

Often a writer can make the meaning of a technical term clear in a word, phrase, or short sentence. Sometimes the definition requires a longer explanation. For example, under some circumstances, the dictionary definition of *psychoanalysis* might be adequate: "a technical procedure for investigating unconscious mental processes and for treating psychoneuroses." However, Freud, the originator of psychoanalysis, in a lecture to people who knew little about psychology, defined it in the following way.

PASSAGE FOR STUDY

Definition of Psychoanalysis[1]

In psychoanalytic treatment nothing happens but an exchange of words between the patient and the physician. The patient talks, tells of his past experiences, and present impressions, complains, and expresses his wishes and emotions. The physician listens, attempts to direct the patient's thought processes, reminds him, forces his attention in certain directions, gives him explanations and observes the reactions of understanding or denial thus evoked. . . .

The dialogue which constitutes the analysis will admit of no audience; the process cannot be demonstrated. One could, of course, exhibit a neurasthenic or hysterical patient to students at a psychiatric lecture. He would relate his case and his symptoms, but nothing more. He will make the communications necessary to the analysis only under the conditions of a special affective relationship to the physician; in the presence of a single person to whom he was indifferent he would become mute. For these communications relate to all his most private thoughts and feelings, all that which as a socially independent person he must hide from others, all that which, being foreign to his own conception of himself, he tries to conceal even from himself.

▶ **Exercise 1**

1. Give one circumstance in which the dictionary definition of *psychoanalysis* would be appropriate and sufficient.
2. What type of information do you get from Freud's definition of the term *psychoanalysis* that was missing in the dictionary definition?
3. Is the vocabulary in these definitions equally difficult? Explain.

---

[1] Reprinted from *A General Introduction to Psychoanalysis* by Sigmund Freud, with the permission of Liveright Publishing Corporation. Copyright 1920 by Edward L. Bernays. Copyright renewed © 1963 by Joan Riviere.

4. Discuss what dictionary definitions attempt to do and what dictionary definitions cannot do because of lack of space.
5. Lesson 11 presented ways to develop an idea. Which of these ways did Freud use in defining *psychoanalysis?* What other methods could he have used?

▶ **Exercise 2**

Choose a technical term that is not commonly understood. Explain its meaning in such simple terms that one not acquainted with the field can understand. You may need to tell what it is *not,* in order to distinguish it from similar things with which it may be confused. You may need to classify it or tell about its characteristics. You may need to indicate the meaning of other technical words you are forced to use in order to explain this term.

Here are suggested topics, but you may want to choose another:

conditioned reflex	extemporaneous speech	id
sentence melody	genetics	isotope
anapestic meter	cybernetics	osmosis
law of supply and demand	sound wave	epic poem

PASSAGE FOR STUDY (Purposely not paragraphed)

Definition of a Paragraph

Authors of textbooks on writing sooner or later come to a discussion of the paragraph. Visually, a paragraph is that part of a composition which occurs between one indentation from the margin and another indentation.[2] But, one asks, what is the reason for the indentation? How does a writer know when to start a new paragraph? Let us begin to answer this question by examining two assertions about a paragraph. James M. McCrimmon says, "In short, a paragraph is an essay in miniature,"[3] while W. Ross Winterowd says,

[2] In some instances, such as in business letters, paragraphs are often signaled by double spacing between lines rather than by indentation.
[3] James M. McCrimmon, *Writing with a Purpose, A First Course in College Composition,* 4th ed. (Cambridge, Mass.: Houghton Mifflin, 1967), p. 109.

"A paragraph is not an essay in miniature."[4] In view of such contradictory statements, can we arrive at a working definition of a paragraph which will help us in writing our own compositions? Can we understand why these authors made such contradictory statements and extract the value from each definition? Let us begin by examining Winterowd's definition: "A paragraph is not an essay in miniature." If we look through any book, magazine, or newspaper written in English, we will find paragraphs that consist of only one or two sentences—and sometimes only a word or a phrase. We can surely agree that one or two sentences cannot constitute a composition—even in miniature—because one or two sentences cannot develop any idea to the extent we expect in a composition. If we read the selection in which such paragraphs occur, we find that these short paragraphs are used either (1) to relate what has preceded to what will follow (i.e., they are transition paragraphs) or (2) to give dramatic force to a given idea. Another thing we notice about these short paragraphs is that they occur only occasionally. Most transitional phrases and sentences occur at the beginning of a longer paragraph, not as a separate paragraph. Furthermore, giving dramatic emphasis to an idea by putting it in a separate paragraph is a device that cannot be used often without defeating its purpose. So we can conclude that, although some paragraphs are transitions and some are used for dramatic effect, these are not typical of most paragraphs. They do, however, present a single point, and because of indentation, they look like paragraphs; therefore they have to be classed as paragraphs. We can, therefore, understand one reason why Winterowd says that paragraphs (*all* paragraphs) are not miniature compositions. If we exclude these occasional paragraphs and consider only the longer, more common type of paragraph, what can we agree on about the content of each? McCrimmon says, "A paragraph requires the same process of composition as a whole essay, though in smaller scope," and Winterowd states that "normal movement of paragraphs is from general statements to more and more specific working out of those statements." Though McCrimmon's statement is more general, both authors seem to feel that ideas in a paragraph are related in some special kind of way. Might we then conclude that perhaps Winterowd and McCrimmon are not as far apart in their conception of what a paragraph contains as the original defini-

---

[4] W. Ross Winterowd, *Structure, Language and Style* (Dubuque, Iowa: Brown, 1969), p. 45.

tions would lead us to believe? Could we say that most paragraphs develop some unifying idea which may be stated specifically or may be only implied? Visually, a paragraph is generally signaled either by indentation or by a change of spacing between lines.

▶ **Exercise 3**

1. The preceding definition of a paragraph has not been sectioned into paragraphs. What are the disadvantages of unparagraphed material?
2. On the basis of what you already knew or have learned from reading the definition of a paragraph, indicate by slash marks [/] how the preceding selection should be paragraphed. Discuss the paragraphing with your classmates.
3. The College Edition of the *Random House Dictionary of the English Language* defines a paragraph as "a distinct portion of written or printed matter, dealing with a particular idea, usually beginning with an indentation on a new line." What aspects of this definition are discussed at more length in the longer definition? Why?
4. In what sentence does the writer reveal why the definitions of McCrimmon and Winterowd are presented? By what other means could the author of this passage have defined the word *paragraph?*
5. Discuss how a single paragraph is different from—and how like—an essay. Use paragraphs from this textbook or from others to prove your points.

Comparison

Comparison is often used effectively to explain a complex point in terms of something that the reader knows. If a reader can picture what he does not understand in terms of what he does understand, it helps him to see the new process or principle or situation more clearly. Of course it is important that the things being compared are actually comparable. It would be of little use (as well as impossible) to explain the organization of a government by comparing it to a gasoline engine.

PASSAGE FOR STUDY

The Voices of the Strings[5]

The violin commands a variety of effects of which no other instrument is capable. Its lovely voice can be now tender and caressing, now torn with heart-rending lamentation, or bursting forth in impassioned, lyrical song. The *viola* is the instrument whose voice was born changed. It is the alto of the section, played under the chin as is the violin, but larger in size. It gives forth a sombre, deep-bodied tone, rich and sonorous like the voice of Marian Anderson. From ten to twelve instruments comprise the viola section. The *violon-cello,* usually abbreviated 'cello, is the baritone in this string choir. The 'cello is a good deal larger than the viola, has longer, thicker strings, and is clutched between the knees. A favorite pastime of the irreverent is to watch for it to skid during a concert. Its rubber tip, or pin, however, is frequently anchored in a convenient crack in the flooring. The masculine 'cello has a rich, mellow, resonant, majestic tone. There are usually ten 'cellos in the orchestra. The strings of the *double bass,* also called *bass viol,* the grandfather of the family, are thick as ropes. The tones of the bass viols are unmistakable, they are so deep, and rich, and vibrating. The old-time name for the violin in English-speaking countries is fiddle; and the bass viol, because of its size and masculinity of tone is known, quite appropriately, as the bull fiddle. Six of these giant instruments are usually found in the orchestra. Only rarely are the bass viols fortunate enough to play a complete melody; their main function is to furnish a foundation for the orchestra.

▶ **Exercise 4**

In explaining the composition of the string section of the orchestra, Syd Skolsky compares it to human voices: the violin to the soprano, the viola to the alto, the cello to the baritone, and the bass viol to the bass. Underline the phrases or sentences that keep the reader aware of this comparison, and be prepared to read them to the class.

---

[5] Syd Skolsky, *Evenings with Music* (New York: Dutton, 1944), pp. 19–20.

▶ **Exercise 5**

The preceding passage for study is part of a chapter furnishing information for people who want a basic foundation for musical listening. Here the author has described the string section of the orchestra. Suggest what the rest of the chapter is about.

Contrast

Comparison, as we have seen, is a means of pointing out similarities; contrast emphasizes differences. While comparison is a common way of making a point clear, contrast is used just as often and just as effectively. A good example is Lev Vygotsky's explanation of the differences between a human being's learning to speak and his learning to write.

PASSAGE FOR STUDY

Differences in the Development of Writing and Speech in the Individual[6]

Our investigation has shown that the development of writing does not repeat the developmental history of speaking. Written speech is a separate linguistic function, differing from oral speech in both structure and mode of functioning. Even its minimal development requires a high level of abstraction. It is speech in thought and image only, lacking the musical, expressive, intonational qualities of oral speech. In learning to write, the child must disengage himself from the sensory aspect of speech and replace words by images of words. Speech that is merely imagined and that requires symbolization of the sound image in written signs (i.e., a second degree of symbolization) naturally must be as much harder than oral speech for the child as algebra is harder than arithmetic. Our studies show that it is the abstract quality of written language that is the main

---

[6] Reprinted from *Thought and Language* by Lev Vygotsky by permission of The M.I.T. Press, Cambridge, Massachusetts, pp. 99–102. Copyright © 1962 by The Massachusetts Institute of Technology.

stumbling block, not the underdevelopment of small muscles or any other mechanical obstacles.

Writing is also speech without an interlocutor, addressed to an absent or an imaginary person or to no one in particular—a situation new and strange to the child. Our studies show that he has little motivation to learn writing when we begin to teach it. He feels no need for it and has only a vague idea of its usefulness. In conversation, every sentence is prompted by a motive. Desire or need lead to request, question to answer, bewilderment to explanation. The changing motives of the interlocutors determine at every moment the turn oral speech will take. It does not have to be consciously directed—the dynamic situation takes care of that. The motives for writing are more abstract, more intellectualized, further removed from immediate needs. In written speech, we are obliged to create the situation, to represent it to ourselves. This demands detachment from the actual situation.

Writing also requires deliberate analytical action on the part of the child. In speaking, he is hardly conscious of the sounds he pronounces and quite unconscious of the mental operations he performs. In writing, he must take cognizance of the sound structure of each word, dissect it, and reproduce it in alphabetical symbols, which he must have studied and memorized before. In the same deliberate way, he must put words in a certain sequence to form a sentence. Written language demands conscious work because its relationship to inner speech is different from that of oral speech: The latter precedes inner speech in the course of development, while written speech follows inner speech and presupposes its existence (the act of writing implying a translation from inner speech). But the grammar of thought is not the same in the two cases. One might even say that the syntax of inner speech is the exact opposite of the syntax of written speech, with oral speech standing in the middle.

Inner speech is condensed, abbreviated speech. Written speech is deployed to its fullest extent, more complete than oral speech. Inner speech is almost entirely predicative because the situation, the subject of thought, is always known to the thinker. Written speech, on the contrary, must explain the situation fully in order to be intelligible. The change from maximally compact inner speech to maximally detailed written speech requires what might be called deliberate semantics—deliberate structuring of the web of meaning.

All these traits of written speech explain why its development in the schoolchild falls far behind that of oral speech.

► **Exercise 6**

1. Make an outline of the selection you have just read. Each main point and subpoint will be a statement of contrast. Compare your outline with those of your classmates.

2. Is there any developmental material in this selection (such as examples, figures, etc.)? Can you give any reason for the selection's being composed almost entirely of conclusions (assertions)? The Russian Lev Vygotsky was one of the foremost researchers of the twentieth century in psychology, education, and psychopathology. Would this have any bearing upon the style of his writing?

3. While Vygotsky is discussing here the writing problems of children, do you think his conclusions might apply to adults as well? Be prepared to discuss this. Use the outline you have just prepared as an aid in doing so.

PASSAGE FOR STUDY

The American Frontier[7]

To Americans the word frontier has a meaning quite different from its use in Europe. There the frontier is a stopping place, a place patrolled by guards, where one must show his papers before passing through. But the American frontier has meant freedom, opportunity, room to expand in. It is not a stopping place but an open door, not a place where you must identify yourself, but a place where you can escape identification if you wish, a place where civilization has not established its rigid pattern, where spaces are wide and men can make their own laws.

The feeling that the frontier was there, to the west, even if a man did not choose to go there has always been a conditioning factor in the American temperament. The frontier, in American thought, was a place beyond civilization where nature took over from man and where the evils concocted by human duplicity were washed away by the great rivers, the wide sky, the brisk, clean air.

---

[7] From *Why We Behave Like Americans* by Bradford Smith. Copyright © 1957 by Bradford Smith. Reprinted by permission of J. B. Lippincott Company.

1. Since the selection "The American Frontier" appears in a book written for Americans, why do you think Bradford Smith, the author, considered a definition of the word *frontier* necessary? What are similar words that *you* might need to define if you were writing a book about *your* country for *Americans?* These will probably be words that Americans do not know at all or about which they have wrong conceptions.

2. How does the author use comparison to make his points clear? How does he use contrast?

3. Take one of the words you chose in the first question in this exercise and tell what use you might make of comparison and contrast in your definition.

4. You have probably discovered that English speakers do not have equivalent vocabulary for some word or words that you consider important. Write a paragraph or two in which you define a term that you would like to make clear to speakers of English. Take advantage of the planning that you have just done in parts 1 and 3 of this exercise.

Explanation

Sometimes explanation is required to make clear what we want to say. Note here how Carl Becker uses explanation to make clear what he means by the word *history*.

PASSAGE FOR STUDY

History[8]

(1) I ought first of all to explain that when I use the term *history* I mean knowledge of history. (2) No doubt throughout all past time there actually occurred a series of events which, whether we know what it was or not, constitutes history in some ultimate sense. (3) Nevertheless, much the greater part of these events we can know nothing about, not even that they occurred; many of them

---

[8] Carl Becker, "Everyman His Own Historian," *The American Historical Review,* January 1932, 221–222. Reprinted with permission of the editor.

we can know only imperfectly; and even the few events that we think we know for sure we can never be absolutely certain of, since we can never revive them, never observe or test them directly. (4) The event itself once occurred, but as an actual event it has disappeared; so that in dealing with it the only objective reality we can observe or test is some material trace which the event has left—usually a written document. (5) With these traces of vanished events, these documents, we must be content since they are all we have; from them we infer what the event was, we affirm that it is a fact that the event was so and so. (6) We do not say, "Lincoln is assassinated"; we say, "It is a fact that Lincoln was assassinated." (7) The event *was,* but is no longer; it is only the affirmed fact about the event that *is,* that persists, and will persist until we discover that our affirmation is wrong or inadequate. (8) Let us then admit that there are two histories: the actual series of events that once occurred; and the ideal series that we affirm and hold in memory. (9) The first is absolute and unchanged—it was what it was whatever we do or say about it; the second is relative, always changing in response to the increase or refinement of knowledge. (10) The two series correspond more or less; it is our aim to make the correspondence as exact as possible; but the actual series of events exists for us only in terms of the ideal series which we affirm and hold in memory. (11) This is why I am forced to identify history with knowledge of history. (12) For all practical purposes history is, for us and for the time being, what we know it to be.

▶ **Exercise 8**

1. In the preceding selection "The Meaning of History" the author wants to explain what the word *history* means to him. Why is it necessary that he do this?
2. Why is a one-sentence definition or the use of synonyms not sufficient to accomplish the author's purpose?
3. Does the first sentence furnish a clue as to the means the author intends to use to make clear the meaning of the word *history?*
4. Where in the selection does the author give a one-sentence definition of history? Does he give it more than once? Why or why not?
5. What is the function of sentences 8 through 12 in relation to the rest of the passage?

► **Exercise 9**

Note the methods by which the ideas in the paragraph on history are related to each other: by repetition of a term (sentence 2, "a series of *events*"; sentence 3, "these *events*"), by pronoun reference (sentence 8, "*two* histories"; sentence 9, "*The first* is . . ."), and by transitional words and sentence connectors (sentence 3, "Nevertheless"; sentence 4, "but"). Analyze the passage for other transitional devices by answering the following questions.

1. How does the author relate sentence 5 to sentence 4? Sentence 6 to sentence 5? Sentence 7 to sentence 6?
2. What word relates sentence 8 to everything that has been said up to that point?
3. How are sentences 11 and 12 related to sentence 1? How does the author make this relationship clear?

Restatement

Restatement is not repetition. *Restatement is repeating the idea in different words.* We use restatement sometimes because when we first express an idea, we realize immediately that some readers may not understand the vocabulary we used. Another reason for restating is to give emphasis. W. N. Parrish gives yet another reason for the need to rephrase an idea.

(1) There is a time factor involved in understanding. (2) The clearest possible statement of a matter may not be grasped by the listener because his mind doesn't have time to develop it, unfold it, get a grip on it. (3) If he could have the statement before him in print so that he could reread it and study it, he might readily come to understand it. (4) And often the full import and implication of a statement is not grasped at once because the listener needs time to relate it and compare it with what he knows. (5) If a significant thought is thrown at him like a sudden dash of water, it may splash off without wetting the surface of his mind. It takes time for some things to soak in.[9]

---

[9] Reprinted by permission of Charles Scribner's Sons from *Speaking in Public* by W. M. Parrish. Copyright 1947 Charles Scribner's Sons.

1. What is the reason Parrish gives for the use of restatement?
2. Parrish is discussing the need for restatement *in public speaking.* What sentences tell you that?
3. In what sentences does Parrish use restatement to make his point clear?
4. Would you conclude that restatement is desirable in writing as well as in speaking? Why or why not?
5. Why might there be a difference in the amount or kind of restatement needed in the two media of communication?

Composition

In this assignment, outline your material before writing to assure the quality of the overall structure of your composition. Then when you have planned the major pattern of your thought and start to plan the development of ideas, be aware of opportunities to make the ideas clearer and more vivid by the use of comparison, contrast, or one of the other methods you have just studied. In the finished theme note in the margin instances where you have used these devices.

A. Choose a term from the following list of abstract words, each of which may mean different things to different people. Explain the meaning of this term as you use it. For example, if you write about *the good life,* you would need to ask yourself what things about life mean most to you. Do you value personal relationships, security, a feeling of accomplishment, freedom, aesthetic experiences? Such topics will probably form your main points, but in the space of a two- or three-page theme, you will not have time to develop adequately more than two or three topics; narrow your discussion to the most important.

home	free speech	character
the good life	personality	a friend
a classic	culture	democracy
idealism	a hero	a liberal
a good meal	literature	thinking

B. For a student, reading is an important part of life. Choose one of the following aspects of reading to develop into a composition. If none of these sparks your interest, narrow the subject of reading in some other way, and write a composition about it.

1. Is there a magazine or newspaper that you intend to subscribe to for many years to come? Give your reasons.
2. Explain how some book or play has influenced your moral or spiritual ideas and beliefs. Tell what characters, events, or philosophical comments have impressed you.
3. Do you think a person can be well educated and not know how to read? Explain why or why not. Give evidence to prove your point. Opinion is not convincing unless accompanied by evidence.
4. If a disaster by some chance destroyed all but five books in the world, what books do you hope would be saved, and why?
5. Did literature courses in high school or preparatory school increase, decrease, or not appreciably affect your interest in reading? Explain the reasons for your answer.
6. What are the values of reading history? Biography? Philosophy? Novels? Poetry? Plays? Choose one form and explain your answers.
7. Should the things that men and women read be somewhat different? Explain why you answer as you do.
8. Are there advantages to reading aloud? To someone? To oneself? Are there disadvantages?
9. How are two given magazines or books alike and how do they differ?
10. What is the best way to treat a book? Should a person "respect" his books by taking good care of them—and what is involved in taking good care of them? If he considers it useful, should the owner of a book feel free to underline, make marginal notes, keep a personal index at the end, and so on?
11. Does the lending of books present a problem to you? What rules have you devised for books you lend? How do you get them back? What do you have to know about a person before you lend books to him? How do you proceed when you borrow a book?

Organizing the Composition
Cause-Effect Order; Problem-Solution Order

Cause-Effect Order

We have seen in Lesson 12 how ideas can be arranged in time order, space order, or topical order. Another way to arrange ideas in sequence is to discuss causes and then the effects that may result from these causes. This order may also be reversed: We may start by describing the result and then inquire into the causes.

PASSAGE FOR STUDY

The Influence of the American Frontier

In the United States we find a teeming nation of people derived from all corners of the world and bound together in a federal system of government. To understand how such a diverse mass of people— originally speaking different languages and adhering to different customs and religions—could eventually develop common character- istics that distinguish them from the people of other nations of the world, we must understand the influence of the frontier on the development of the country. The frontier, according to Frederick Jackson Turner, one of the great historians of the United States, was the greatest single influence in shaping what America was to become.

Frontier life followed several patterns. During the period of the settlement of the United States, the frontier meant the end of a populated area and the beginning of land open to all. For four hundred years—from the discovery of America until the last quarter of the nineteenth century—there was a geographic frontier which kept moving westward. The first Europeans established colonies on the Atlantic Coast, and beyond those settlements was the first frontier. In the seventeenth century pioneers followed the rivers to the Appalachian Mountains, and the mountains became the frontier. During the Revolutionary War, Americans crossed the Allegheny section of those mountains. By 1820 settlements were found along the banks of the Ohio River, clear to the Mississippi, and down the Mississippi to Louisiana. Settlements had advanced into Kansas and Nebraska by 1850. Then gold was discovered in California. Pioneers passed beyond the Great Plains and Rocky Mountains, headed for the West Coast. Finally, in the last quarter of the nineteenth century, the plains and mountains were settled, and the last geographic frontier of the United States was no more.

The settlement of each new section of the country followed a consistent pattern. Explorers and fur traders were the first white men to enter each new region, and they advanced rapidly. The trade between the Indians and Europeans was satisfactory to both parties, but the Indians could not foresee that after the traders other forces of civilization were to come which would change their traditional way of life. Miners and ranchers followed close upon the heels of the explorers and traders. Eventually farmers arrived, and the settlement of the country was complete.

As America developed, each new section in turn displayed a pattern of advance from a primitive society to a highly organized one. Conditions of frontier living and the evolution of the frontier had a profound effect upon the character of the individual and upon the nation.

How did it affect the individual? At first the frontier reduced all comers to the level of a primitive society. Whatever corner of the earth a man came from, no matter what his station or wealth in another society, the frontier made the same demands of each one. A man had to stand or fall on his ability to cope with the problems it presented: the land, the weather, Indian attacks. He had to be his own law, his own doctor, his own priest. So the frontier was the great leveler of social and national barriers. It made immigrants into a new breed of men who relied on their own resourcefulness and inventiveness.

Loneliness on the frontier played its part, too, in shaping American character. In the vast spaces, the explorer, the trader, the miner, the stockman, and the farmer were alone for long periods of time. Another human being was a welcome sight. Anyone passing through the country was urged not only to spend the night but to stay for days. When settlers left their homes to go for supplies—journeys which sometimes took many days—they often left their cabin doors unlocked, and any traveler was welcome to come in and cook what food he could find. Thus Americans developed a naive friendliness and belief in the goodness of others. Visitors from abroad are sometimes baffled by the instant heartiness with which Americans meet them, because it seems to imply more friendship than a quick meeting can bring. This immediate friendliness is a legacy of the frontier where one did not have time for friendships to ripen slowly. The frontier helped determine what the average American would become.

It also determined what the nation was to become. An American's allegiance to his state and city and to the place he calls home is strong; yet he considers the national government supreme over the states in some matters. The long tradition of frontier life conditioned him to accept a dual loyalty. The frontiersman, without telephone, telegraph, or railroad, developed a loyalty to his little world. On the other hand, there were certain ways in which frontier communities were forced to join with each other. Even so small a matter as the need for salt tied frontiersmen to the rest of the country. The yearly journeys that the settlers made back to civilization to get salt are one example. Frontiersmen similarly were dependent on the national government for internal improvements such as railroads and the telegraph, for a system of disposition of public lands, and for tariffs to protect the price of their agricultural products and the products of their struggling new industries. Thus, regional loyalty came to exist side by side with recognition of the need for and loyalty to a federal authority.

Today the geographic frontier of the United States is gone. If the individual becomes annoyed with the conditions of an increasingly complex society, there is no open country beyond the borders to which he can flee. But four hundred years of frontier life have left their stamp on the country—on the attitudes and personality of the individual, on the state, and on the nation. The frontier has become a symbol for great challenge and great reward, for starting a new way of life. As such it has been used in the titles of books, in the names of organizations, and in political campaigns. One of

the most recent uses was John F. Kennedy's labeling of his plans
for improving the nation "the New Frontier."

▶ **Exercise 1**

Here is an incomplete outline of "The Influence of the American Frontier." After you have studied it, answer the questions
that follow.

Thesis sentence: The frontier was the greatest single influence
in shaping what America was to become.

  I. Frontier life followed several patterns.
    A. There was a geographic pattern.
       1.
       2.
       3.
       4.
       5.
       6.
    B. There was a pattern of advance from a primitive
       society to a highly organized one.
  II. The frontier affected the nation.
    A. It affected the individual.
       1.
       2.
    B. It affected the type of government that the United
       States has.
       1.
       2.

Answer the following questions about the preceding outline:

1. What is the overall plan of organization; that is, what is the
   relationship between the ideas expressed in points I and II?
2. In complete sentences, fill in the subpoints under I, A (There
   was a geographic pattern.) Are these subpoints arranged according to time, space, or topic?
3. What is the pattern of organization of the subpoints under main
   point II?
4. If this selection about the American frontier were expanded,
   what points do you feel should be developed more fully? Which

of the following means of development would you like to see used, and where?

description	facts	a line of reasoning
examples	figures	comparison and contrast
illustration	definition	quotation from authority

Problem-Solution Order

Mankind is always having to solve problems: religious, economic, political, educational, health, problems precipitated by personal relationships, and so on. The famous problem-solving sequence of John Dewey (adapted from the methods of scientific experimentation) presents a basic patterning of thought commonly encountered in writing and reading. The sequence involves the following steps:

1. Defining the problem, or giving evidence that the problem exists
2. Studying the causes of the problem
3. Suggesting possible solutions to the problem
4. Picking a solution that seems most promising, and explaining why it seems so

Such a problem-solution sequence is useful in organizing term papers and theses, or might well serve as a basis for a series of compositions or speeches. Following are some suggestions for developing each step in the sequence.

A. Definition of the problem

Here you tell how you know that a situation exists that calls for action. Who are affected? How are they affected? Is the problem becoming more acute? In the definition of the problem, you often describe conditions or use explanations to make your point clear. For some subjects you will need facts and figures. You may want to make use of examples and illustrations so that your reader can picture the conditions. Again, you may want to contrast present conditions with past conditions.

B. Causes of the problem

Here you tell why the conditions exist. Are several causes operating at the same time? Or is one cause produced by another that comes about because of yet another condition, in a kind of chain reaction? For example, suppose a certain college does not have adequate library facilities. Its facilities are not adequate because of increased enrollment. Its enrollment is increased because more people have money to go to college because wages are high. Wages are high because—and so forth. Operating simultaneously is another cause of the problem: The income of the college has not increased in proportion to increased enrollment.

C. Possible solutions to the problem

Many problems that one might discuss have no simple or easy solution. The best that one can hope to do is to point out areas in which improvement has been made and in which further improvement might be brought about if certain things were done. The suggestions must seem practical and reasonable. One way to discover solutions is to find ways to eliminate the causes. Common questions that are often ignored are how the proposed solutions are to be financed and how adequate personnel can be provided to get the job done. Such practical matters are of great importance.

▶ Exercise 2

Here are skeleton outlines for a sequence of three compositions on the problems that occur in giving and grading college examinations. The first theme will define the problem by giving evidence that it exists, the second composition will investigate the causes of the problem, and the last composition will suggest possible solutions to the problem. After you have studied these outlines, do the exercise that follows them.

Composition I: Definition of the problem

Thesis sentence: There is evidence that there are problems involved in giving and grading final examinations in college.

  I. Students regularly protest about their grades on examinations.
    A.
    B.
 II.
 III.

Composition II: Causes of the problem

Thesis sentence: Here are reasons why both college students and instructors are dissatisfied with the present administering of final examinations.

    I. An examination cannot test a student's knowledge of all the material presented in a course.
       A.
       B.
       C.
  II.
       A.
       B.
 III.

Composition III: Possible solutions to the problem

Thesis sentence: Although the problems inherent in giving and grading final examinations cannot be solved entirely, these are suggestions that may lessen the difficulties somewhat.

    I. Some weeks before the examination is given, students could be furnished a list of review questions covering important material from which the examination questions would be taken.
  II.

A. Following are some statements of main points (marked in an outline by I, II, III) that belong in the preceding outlines. Put each of the main points into the outline in which it belongs. This is a test to see whether you can recognize the difference between definition or evidence of a problem, the causes of a problem, and the solutions to a problem.

1. Even a top-ranking student in a class may have emotional problems at examination time.
2. In some examinations most of the class may get a failing grade.
3. Some students are fatigued at examination time and thus cannot do their best, particularly in examinations at the end of final examination week.

4. Students in an examination could be given a number of questions from which to choose those they felt best qualified to answer.
5. Sometimes students who go into a final examination with top grades in a course get a low grade in the final examination.

B. Here are subpoints (marked A, B, and C on the outline) that support the main points in the three preceding outlines. Put each subpoint in its proper place under a main point in the appropriate outline.

1. They protest to their instructors.
2. The time limit of a test results in questions that cover only part of the material.
3. The questions are selected by a teacher who may not choose them wisely.
4. Students protest to other students.
5. Even if wisely chosen, examination questions may not elicit from a student what he has learned in the course; yet his grade is supposed to reflect exactly that.

▶ Exercise 3

Here are skeleton outlines with thesis sentences and main points for a sequence of compositions that explore the existence of a problem, its causes, and its solution. You will note that all of the main points are assertions that need to be developed with subpoints giving specific material. Supply appropriate types of developmental material in the blanks in each outline. Since you are not expected to do the library research it would require to support these assertions with real facts and figures, furnish imaginary facts, figures, examples, and so on, that seem appropriate. *Imaginary developmental material* such as you will use is given in points A, B, and C under point I in the first outline.

Outline I: Definition of the problem

Thesis sentence: The supply of nurses in our community is inadequate.

  I. Doctors have an inadequate number of well-trained nurses in their offices.

	A. A report issued by the Department of Health, Education and Welfare states that only 25 percent of the doctors in the United States have in their offices nurses with Registered Nurse (R.N.) certificates.
Imaginary Supporting Material	B. Quote my own doctor (Dr. Smith), who says he could handle at least five to ten more patients a day if he had more nurses to give shots, take blood samples, and so on.
	C. Give the example of Dr. White, in a small rural town in Arkansas, who has difficulty in keeping even one nurse in his office.

II. Patients in hospitals need more care than they are now receiving.
   A.
   B.
   C.

Outline II: Causes of the problem

Thesis sentence: There are several reasons why the supply of well-trained nurses in the United States is inadequate.

I. With increased income, more people can afford care by trained nurses.
   A.
   B.
   C.

II. With improved health conditions, people live longer and there are more elderly people who require competent nursing care.
   A.
   B.
   C.

III. Nursing as a profession has not attracted young men and women in large enough numbers to keep up with the demand.
   A.
   B.
   C.

Outline III: Possible solutions to the problem

Thesis sentence: There are several solutions one might propose to lessen the problem of the inadequate number of nurses in the United States.

   I. Lower the standards of admission to nursing training programs in order to increase the number of trainees.
     A.
     B.
     C.
  II. Attract more nurses by raising the prestige of nursing as a profession.
     A.
     B.
 III. Persuade communities to contribute to scholarships for nursing training programs.
     A.
     B.

Outline IV: The defense of one solution to the problem

Thesis sentence: To lessen the problem of an insufficient number of nurses in the United States, we need to increase the prestige of nursing by upgrading standards in the nursing schools.

   I. Better nursing will be provided if nursing school standards are upgraded.
     A.
     B.
  II. High-caliber young men and women will be attracted in greater numbers to a profession of high standing.
     A.
     B.

Composition

Do each of the following three assignments.

A. "The Influence of the American Frontier" at the beginning of this lesson was written to help you understand American society as well as to point out certain things about organizing your compositions. In this assignment, choose a topic that will help others understand the people of your country. Explain some social custom, some institution, or some type of development in your country (the effect) and discuss what produced it (the cause). If a person from the United States were writing on this topic he might discuss service clubs, medical clinics, homes for old people, counseling programs in colleges, or the growth of the house-trailer industry. Other countries have other types of customs and development. When you have finished writing your first draft, do the following:

1. Check the manuscript for spelling and punctuation errors.
2. Make sure that you have used a clear transition between the presentation of the result and the presentation of the causes.
3. Look over each sentence and make sure that you have used the simple present tense of the verb in all places where it should be used.

B. Choose a problem that exists in your country (social, health, economic, education). This problem should be one of general interest to people in your country, not just to yourself. This problem will serve as the basis for a series of four composition assignments, so it should be a significant one with which you have had some first-hand experience and preferably one on which you can do research in the library. Develop a composition based on each stage of the problem-solving sequence in this lesson. In the first essay you will discuss evidences of the problem; in the second essay you will discuss causes of the same problem, and so on. Before you write the essays, prepare an outline for each that includes a statement of specific purpose and introductory and concluding remarks as well as the subject sentence and main points, as illustrated in the outlines you went over earlier in this lesson. Your compositions will be checked particularly for the following points:

1. Whether your central idea (subject sentence) is clear
2. Whether your main points clearly relate to each other and to the subject sentence

3. Whether you present sufficient developmental material to make your points clear

C. Before you write any one composition in the preceding exercise you may want to present your ideas to your classmates in a five-minute speech. They will discuss with you whether your central idea and main points were clearly expressed and whether you developed each point sufficiently.

Organizing the Composition *Deductive and Inductive Order; Writing Essay Examinations*

In all of the kinds of rhetorical patterns we have studied so far (time, space, topical, cause-effect, problem-solution), the pattern has been determined by the relationship of the main points to each other. We now come to two kinds of rhetorical order that are not based on the relationship among the main points. Deductive order and inductive order reflect the relative placement of the thesis sentence and the main points. In deductive order the writer states his thesis, then develops it; in inductive order he develops his ideas and states his thesis at the end. The nature of the subject, the reader, and the situation—all are factors in determining which type of order is best for a given piece of writing.

Note that inductive and deductive order of arrangement of ideas are quite different concepts from inductive and deductive reasoning. The similarity in vocabulary is unfortunate, and sometimes confusing to students.

Deductive Order

Deductive order is by far the most common order in expository writing. It is an aid to both the writer and the reader. By stating the thesis at the outset, a writer is more likely to keep to the subject and relate the main points to the central idea as well as to each other. When the thesis sentence is found at the beginning of a book or a chapter, a composition or a paragraph, it is in an expected place and often saves a researcher's time as well as helping any reader get oriented.

One of the important uses of deductive order is in writing essay examinations, which will be discussed at the end of this lesson.

PASSAGE FOR STUDY

Magnanimity[1]

(1) Virtues exist in action. (2) Let us have a look at a few examples of magnanimity as it has been lived. (3) The first is a Scotsman, not because of the patriotism of this occasion, but because through all the Amazonian undergrowth of literary history, he stands out as a man, generous and good. (4) I am thinking of Sir Walter Scott. (5) He was not, I suppose, one of the greatest novelists, though he was very much better than he is at present considered to be, and was one of the most influential who have ever lived. (6) But in his life, in his relations with other writers, in the way he took both enormous triumph and fantastic disaster, he sets a standard which ought to make the rest of us ashamed. (7) If a fraction of the world's intellectual persons came anywhere near the goodness of Walter Scott, then the world would be a better place. (8) Ask me to choose a personification of magnanimity from all the world's writers, and I think I should take him.

(9) My next is Turgenev. . . . (10) Turgenev had great literary success young, and in fact remained successful all his life. (11) He was ten years older than Tolstoi, and when they first met, Turgenev was the most distinguished writer in Russia, and Tolstoi a beginner. (12) Fairly soon, that position changed. (13) Tolstoi published *War and Peace* when he was in his late thirties, and was, with surprising speed, recognized as the first novelist not only of Russia, but of the world. (14) Turgenev was not simply a fine writer. (15) He was a man of acute critical perception. (16) He knew, and said, that this estimate was just. (17) It cannot have been easy. (18) Turgenev had lived for his art more than most

---

[1] C. P. Snow, "On Magnanimity." Copyright 1962 by Harper's Magazine. Reprinted from the July 1962 issue by special permission.

men—much more than Tolstoi had—and it cost him great suffering to admit that he had been surpassed. (19) And yet his heart was large enough. (20) As he was dying, he wrote Tolstoi one of the most moving letters in all literature, begging him to return to writing novels, calling him "greatest writer of the Russian land."

▶ Exercise 1

1. Why is deductive order better than inductive order for this material?
2. In what sentence or sentences does the author let the reader know the point of his two examples? If the two paragraphs on magnanimity had been a complete essay instead of just a portion of a larger article, how could you have changed the first two sentences to make a thesis sentence for the two paragraphs? Is there virtue in having two sentences instead of one to carry the central idea?
3. Compose a fitting concluding paragraph for this selection.

▶ Exercise 2

Although we are focusing our attention in this lesson on matters of organization, good writing is also a matter of being able to present the reader with a sequence of sentences that provide a pleasing balance and variety that appeal to the mind, the eye, and the ear. An expert writer may unconsciously achieve the variety of sentence structure displayed in the preceding selection. The novice must vary his sentence structure consciously. Answer the following questions about the sentence structure in the passage on magnanimity, and then as you write your own compositions try to incorporate in them some of the aspects of Snow's sentence structure that are effective.

1. Why is a short first sentence effective in this passage?
2. In which sentences does the writer repeat sentence elements effectively? What elements are repeated?
3. Would a sentence containing similarly repeated elements have been effective immediately following this one?
4. How many sentences in the paragraph are stated as commands

or requests? Where are these sentences placed? Why is this placement effective?

▶ **Exercise 3**

Following is a paragraph written in deductive order. The first and last sentences have been omitted. After the passage, the first and last sentences are given. Read the paragraph and be prepared to tell which sentence was the introductory sentence and which was the concluding one.

Linguistic Change[2]

(1) . . . (2) If we could imagine the impossible—a society in which nothing happened—there would be no changes in language. (3) But except possibly in a cemetery, things are constantly happening to people: they eat, drink, sleep, talk, make love, meet strangers, struggle against natural perils, and fight against one another. (4) They slowly adapt their language to meet the changing conditions of their lives. (5) Although the changes made in one generation may be small, those made in a dozen generations may enormously affect the language. (6) The big and little phases of history—fashions, fads, inventions, the influence of a leader, a war or two, travel to a foreign land, the demands of a business intercourse—may alter a language so much that a Rip Van Winkle who slept two or three hundred years might have trouble in making himself understood when he awoke. (7) . . .

Indicate which of the following sentences is sentence (1) in the paragraph of "Linguistic Change" and which is sentence (7) and explain the reason for your choice:

A language changes because things happen to people.
Even in a relatively quiet society, linguistic change proceeds inexorably.

Inductive Arrangement

A common use of exposition is to explain a point of view. While this use of exposition may result in persuasion, its primary

---

[2] J. N. Hook and E. G. Mathews, *Modern American Grammar and Usage.* Copyright © 1956 The Ronald Press Company, New York.

purpose is to give reasons, and it makes use of the devices of arrangement and support of ideas, which we have been studying in previous lessons.

The attitude that you anticipate in the reader affects whether you proceed inductively or deductively. If you think your reader will have no quarrel with your conclusion, you will probably proceed deductively, stating your conclusions at the outset. If you think that your reader will be hostile to your conclusion, you give your reasons first, hoping that he will agree with them one by one until he has to reach the conclusion that you did.

In the passage that follows, notice how Aldo Leopold uses inductive order to bring you to his conclusion.

PASSAGE FOR STUDY

Thinking Like a Mountain[3]

(1) A deep chesty bawl echoes from rimrock to rimrock, rolls down the mountain, and fades into the far blackness of the night. It is an outburst of wild defiant sorrow, and of contempt for all the adversities of the world.

(2) Every living thing (and perhaps many a dead one as well) pays heed to that call. To the deer it is a reminder of the way of all flesh, to the pine a forecast of midnight scuffles and of blood upon the snow, to the coyote a promise of gleanings to come, to the cowman a threat of red ink at the bank, to the hunter a challenge of fang against bullet. Yet behind these obvious and immediate hopes and fears there lies a deeper meaning, known only to the mountain itself. Only the mountain has lived long enough to listen objectively to the howl of a wolf.

(3) Those unable to decipher the hidden meaning know nevertheless that it is there, for it is felt in all wolf country, and distinguishes that country from all other land. It tingles in the spine of all who hear wolves by night, or who scan their tracks by day. Even without sight or sound of wolf, it is implicit in a hundred small events: the midnight whinny of a pack horse, the rattle of rolling rocks, the bound of a fleeing deer, the way shadows lie under the spruces. Only the ineducable tyro can fail to sense the presence or

[3] Aldo Leopold, *A Sand County Almanac* (New York: Oxford University Press, 1949), pp. 129–132. Copyright © 1949, 1953, 1966 by Oxford University Press, Inc. Reprinted by permission.

absence of wolves, or the fact that mountains have a secret opinion about them.

(4) My own conviction on this score dates from the day I saw a wolf die. We were eating lunch on a high rimrock, at the foot of which a turbulent river elbowed its way. We saw what we thought was a doe fording the torrent, her breast awash in white water. When she climbed the bank toward us and shook out her tail, we realized our error: it was a wolf. A half-dozen others, evidently grown pups, sprang from the willows and all joined in a welcoming mêlée of wagging tails and playful maulings. What was literally a pile of wolves writhed and tumbled in the center of an open flat at the foot of our rimrock.

(5) In those days we had never heard of passing up a chance to kill a wolf. In a second we were pumping lead into the pack, but with more excitement than accuracy: how to aim a steep down-hill shot is always confusing. When our rifles were empty, the old wolf was down, and a pup was dragging a leg into impassable slide-rocks.

(6) We reached the old wolf in time to watch a fierce green fire dying in her eyes. I realized then, and have known ever since, that there was something new to me in those eyes—something known only to her and to the mountain. I was young then, and full of trigger-itch; I thought that because fewer wolves meant more deer, that no wolves would mean hunters' paradise. But after seeing the green fire die, I sensed that neither the wolf nor the mountain agreed with such a view. . . .

(7) Since then I have lived to see state after state extirpate its wolves. I have watched the face of many a newly wolfless mountain, and seen the south-facing slopes wrinkle with a maze of new deer trails. I have seen every edible bush and seedling browsed, first to anaemic desuetude, and then to death. I have seen every edible tree defoliated to the height of a saddlehorn. Such a mountain looks as if someone had given God new pruning shears, and forbidden Him all other exercise. In the end the starved bones of the hoped-for deer herd, dead of its own too-much, bleach with the bones of the dead sage, or molder under the high-lined junipers.

(8) I now suspect that just as a deer herd lives in mortal fear of its wolves, so does a mountain live in mortal fear of its deer. And perhaps with better cause, for while a buck pulled down by wolves can be replaced in two or three years, a range pulled down by too many deer may fail of replacement in as many decades.

(9) So also with cows. The cowman who cleans his range of

wolves does not realize that he is taking over the wolf's job of trimming the herd to fit the range. He has not learned to think like a mountain. Hence we have dustbowls, and rivers washing the future into the sea. . . .

(10) Perhaps this is the hidden meaning in the howl of the wolf, long known among mountains, but seldom perceived among men.

▶ **Exercise 4**

Discuss the following questions about the selection you have just read.

1. What is the purpose of the first two paragraphs?
2. What associations do you have in your mind with deer? With wolves? (What stories have you read, and what experiences have you had with these two kinds of animals? If you were going shooting, which would you be inclined to shoot?)
3. What is the message that Aldo Leopold is trying to give to his reader? At what point in the article does the reader know what the message is? Why is it withheld so long?
4. Give the meaning of each of the following from paragraph 7, and explain how each contributes to the point of view that the author is expressing:
   a. every edible tree defoliated to the height of a saddle horn
   b. the . . . slopes wrinkle with a maze of new deer trails
   c. dead of its own too-much
   d. the high-lined junipers
5. How does the vivid description in this selection present evidence that too many deer are a menace?
6. Do you feel that the author knows what he is talking about? Pick out specific details that convince you.
7. It is obvious that the author did not reveal to the reader the steps in his own reasoning before he wrote this article. He no doubt knew that his reader might be hostile toward his conclusion. Sometimes the order of one's logical thought is not the order in which one would arrange the material for his readers. The author's chain of reasoning might well have started like this: (Supply the missing parts at the end.)

a. Topsoil in the United States is being washed into the sea and much property damage is the result of river floods each spring.
b. Floods occur because the mountains are defoliated.
c. Mountains are defoliated because there are such great numbers of deer.
d. There are such great numbers of deer because _____.
e. There are so few wolves because _____.
f. Conclusion: Even though the farmers may lose some animals, _____.

Composition

A. Choose some belief that you hold that differs from the accepted point of view in your community, your country, your social group, or from those of your classmates. Write a composition in which you try to explain this belief to another, using the following rhetorical devices:

1. If possible make the first sentence a statement that arouses the reader's curiosity without revealing your point of view.
2. In the first part of your composition, state some aspect of your subject that your reader can agree with.
3. Show the reader that you have thought the subject through thoroughly. For a model, note the author's knowledge of the country he was talking about in "Thinking Like a Mountain."
4. Avoid an outright statement of your position, but clearly suggest it in the composition.

B. In a composition, evaluate one of the following:

1. a piece of scientific research
2. a literary work (novel, poem, play)
3. a lecture or debate
4. the architecture of a building
5. a work of art (picture, musical composition or performance, a piece of jewelry, etc.)
6. a television or radio program

Generally, evaluative compositions are ordered deductively. Here are some suggestions for writing such a composition.

Techniques for Writing
an Evaluative Essay

Know your overall impression before you start writing

Nothing is either totally good or totally bad, but generally the critic thinks that it was nearer good than bad or nearer bad than good. He should be sure of his own attitude before he starts writing.

Orient your reader in the introduction

Give introductory information about what you are evaluating. For example, if it is scientific research, who did it? When? Where? Where was it reported? And so on. If it was a speech, who was the speaker, where and when did he speak, who was the audience, and what was the subject? Also in the introduction, acquaint your reader with your point of view toward what you are evaluating.

Acquaint your reader briefly with your subject

In approximately one-fourth the length of your total composition, give the reader a clear picture of what you are evaluating. If you are evaluating a painting, this will be a description of it so that the reader can see it clearly in his mind. If it is an experiment, a speech, or a book, summarize it briefly.

Organize your evaluation under clear headings

In three-fourths of the composition, measure the various aspects of the thing you are evaluating against some standard of perfection. The aspects vary with the type of thing you are evaluating. Here are some common aspects that critics consider.

Scientific Research

1. Was the research on a significant subject? Was it timely? Needed?
2. Was it the result of a justifiable hypothesis?
3. Did the project require controlled conditions? If so, were these maintained?
4. Are the results recorded and interpreted correctly, and are the conclusions justified?

A Speech

1. Was the subject worth talking about? Did the speaker make his subject clear? Was the speaker qualified to speak on his subject?
2. Was the speech organized so that the thought could be followed easily?
3. Did the speaker develop his ideas with enough concrete material to make them clear and convincing and to hold your interest?
4. Was the speech delivered with voice and action that made the ideas clearer and more impressive?

A Literary Work

1. Is the dominating impression of interest and value?
2. How well does the form or structure contribute to the total effect?
3. If the work is a narrative, how do plot, setting, and character help develop the theme?
4. How skillfully does the author use special techniques to achieve his purpose?

A Play

1. Was the characterization convincingly conceived by the playwright? Convincingly executed by the actors?
2. Did the plot contribute to the playwright's purpose?
3. Did the lighting effects, the scenery, the costuming, and the pace contribute to the playwright's purpose?

Support your opinions

Use the forms of support you have studied to convince your reader of the soundness of your evaluation: facts, a line of reasoning, quotation from authority, figures, and so on.

Writing Essay Examinations

Many students write an answer to an essay examination like a jack rabbit startled by a hunter. They begin putting words down on paper before they have collected their wits, before they have planned what they want to say. Here are some suggestions for applying what you have learned in this composition class to the writing of essay examination answers. We must assume, of course, that you know the subject matter.

1. When you receive the examination questions, read all of them before you start to write. Pay special attention to the directions.
   a. Discover whether you are asked to answer all the questions, or whether you are to answer a certain number of them, or to choose alternatives.
   b. If you have a choice of questions, decide at once which ones you feel best qualified to answer. Cross out the numbers of the questions you will omit, so that you will not inadvertently spend time on one you did not intend to answer.
   c. Figure out at this point how much time you have to answer each question. Then as you write, allow yourself equal time for each question. Leave a little space at the end of each answer so that if you finish easy questions in less than the allotted time you can go back and spend the extra time on a difficult question.
2. Before you start to answer a question, read the question carefully to discover exactly what information the instructor is asking for. Look for *key words,* such as the ones that are explained here:

Compare
Emphasize similarities. But in case the instructor is using the word in a general sense, you might mention differences too.

Contrast
Stress differences in things, events, problems.

Criticize or evaluate
In criticizing, express your own judgment—for and against. In evaluating, give the judgment of authorities as well as your own.

Define
Be clear, brief, accurate. Give the limits of the definition. Show how the thing you are defining differs from others in its class.

Describe
Often this means to tell or recount in sequence or story form. Or it may mean to give a description.

Diagram

Give a drawing. Label the parts, with perhaps a brief description.

Discuss

Examine carefully; give reasons for and against in discussion form.

Enumerate or list

These words mean the same thing. Present the points briefly in a list.

Explain

Make clear what is meant. You may want to give reasons for differences in results or opinions.

Justify

Give reasons for conclusions or decisions. Try to convince the reader.

Outline

Organize in outline form with main points and subpoints. The main point here is to classify things in brief form.

Prove

Give logical reasons or evidence that a thing is true.

Relate

Show the connection between two things.

Review or state or summarize

These terms mean much the same thing: to give main points, usually omitting details. A *review* may imply examining a subject critically.

Trace

Describe the development or progress of events from some point in the past; that is, put into chronological order.

3. Plan your answer before you start to write. Rephrase the question in statement form. This statement becomes your topic sentence. On the back of your examination paper jot down key words that remind you of the main points you should discuss.
4. Now you are ready to write. Here are some things to remember:
   a. Include only material that is relevant. Do not waste time telling your instructor things he did not ask for.

b. Make your ideas clear by supporting your generalizations and assertions with details that develop or support them. If possible, cite references (authorities or texts) to support what you say.

c. Avoid one-sentence answers. An essay-type question requires an essay-type answer.

5. Reread your answers at the end of the examination period. Check to see if you have said what you intended to say. You may think of an example or have some important comment that you can insert in the margin or between the lines.

6. Make your paper as readable as possible. Write as legibly as you can. Preferably use a pen, but if you have to use pencil, make sure it has a soft enough lead to make the writing easy to see. Provide enough equipment so that you do not have to spend examination time in borrowing something to write with.

▶ **Exercise on Writing Essay Examinations**

Following are some sample answers to essay examination questions. Some of them contain common errors. One is satisfactory. Be prepared to discuss the shortcomings of each defective answer and decide which answer is satisfactory and why.

Examination question. Discuss the effects of the American frontier upon American life today. (See the first passage for study in the preceding lesson.)

Answer 1: Made people more self-reliant. But they were lonely. Would welcome any stranger. Not like today when we are sometimes suspicious of the stranger who comes to our door. But of course times have changed. There is more crime and so we have reason to be suspicious of strangers. There is no place where we have those same frontier conditions today.

Answer 2: To a student of American history one of the most interesting parts of the study is the development of the frontier— of course we have to keep remembering that the frontier changed and Americans moved farther and farther west in the United States. We have to remember too that there was a distinctive pattern of development of the frontier. First the explorers came and then the traders with the Indians. Then the miners and the ranchers came in to develop the country. Finally, when the farmers arrived, civilization had taken over. But Americans today are a lot like the pioneers in many ways. They are individualistic like him but perhaps not as resourceful. They are not lonely either. But they still greet strangers with the same friendliness that the pioneers did.

Answer 3: The effects of the American frontier on life today are:

1. It made Americans more individualistic.
2. It made Americans more friendly. Americans greet foreigners in a more friendly way than they are greeted by many foreigners.
3. Americans have a dual loyalty—to both state and nation.

Answer 4: The American frontier had at least five important effects upon American life today. On the frontier, men had to rely on themselves to do things. This has resulted today in making Americans more individualistic. A second effect of the frontier was to break down social barriers, and this lack of social barriers still exists. Still another effect was that the loneliness of the frontier, which fostered friendliness toward strangers, left an impression on succeeding generations so that Americans today tend to greet strangers with instant friendliness and a belief in their goodness. A fourth legacy of the frontier is that it gave to Americans a sense of loyalty both to their particular region and to the central government at the same time. Finally, the frontier has always meant a place where a person had to work hard and risk a lot, but it offered a great reward. Therefore, in American thinking, the frontier is a symbol for starting a new way of life.

Writing the Library
Research Paper *Locating Suitable Material; Taking Notes; Integrating the Material into Your Own Composition; Giving Credit for Material Taken from Others*

Often you will be asked to write a paper in which you present the results of your reading about a topic. Your paper may be a summary of information about a subject gained entirely from reading, or you may use facts from your reading to supplement what you already know or to develop or support your own point of view on a topic. Many of the problems in writing such a paper—selecting a topic, narrowing it to suit the scope of your paper, stating the thesis or purpose clearly, organizing the material and developing points adequately—are identical with those that have been discussed so far. There are particular problems in writing, however, that result from the use of library material. They are:

1. Finding suitable sources of information on your subject
2. Extracting pertinent material and taking notes on it
3. Integrating material gained from your reading into your own composition
4. Giving proper credit to your sources

This lesson will not cover in detail every aspect of writing a library research paper but will give you some suggestions on the points just listed.

Finding Suitable Sources of Information

Two problems in finding suitable material are first of all locating books, periodicals, or newspaper articles that contain material pertinent to what you are writing about, and second, finding the facts that you need in the sources that you have gathered.

Locating and using sources

Suggested sources material in American libraries:

1. *Encyclopedias.* Encyclopedia articles are often valuable for a short overview of the entire area. These articles are extremely condensed and cover a wide area without going into great detail. Thus your paper, in which you present a limited area or a particular point of view in some detail, can rarely be based solely on an article in an encyclopedia.

2. Readers' Guide, *or other periodical indexes, or indexes in special subject-matter fields.* The *Readers' Guide* indexes articles from periodicals covering a wide variety of fields. It is brought up to date semimonthly. Articles are listed by author, title, and subject. The subject entries may be most pertinent to your purposes. You may want to consult the reference librarian for special indexes in your field.

3. *Card catalog.* The card catalog indexes books by author, title, and subject. Usually the best way to begin is by looking under the general subject you are writing on. The cards in the catalog generally give the table of contents of books. This may help you in determining whether the book will be of use to you in your paper. Generally, though, if an entire book has been written on the aspect of the subject you are going to write about, the subject is too large for your paper.

4. *File of pamphlets and clippings.* Often the reference librarian can direct you to a file of clippings and other miscellaneous items

that do not appear in the card catalog. This file is also usually in alphabetical order by subject.

5. *Microfilm or microfiche duplications* of articles in various fields. These need to be read in a microfilm reader. Your librarian can tell you where these are located.

6. *Bibliographical lists in books and articles.* An often overlooked source of further material on your subject is the bibliography that often appears at the end of an article or at the end of a chapter of a book.

When using these sources to find material, record the *author, title, publisher,* and *date of publication* of any reference that you think you may use. You will need the information later in making a bibliography and giving credit for material that you used in your paper. See bibliography form, Appendix, p. 259.

Locating pertinent material in your sources

When you have collected a preliminary bibliography of material on your subject, your next problem is to determine what you need to read carefully and possibly take notes on and what you can reject. From the card catalog you may have found chapters of books that you can go to directly. The entire chapter may not serve your purpose, however. Look at the subdivisions of the chapters, if they are indicated; then read the opening and summary paragraphs. The same procedure will also save you time in reading material from periodicals.

▶ Exercise 1

1. Assume that, in a course you are taking, your assignment is to write a term paper based on your reading about some aspect of a topic you are studying in that course. Use one of the following topics, or choose one that might actually develop from a course you are taking now.

music or art	education	language
history	science	anthropology
social reform	literature	

2. Narrow your topic to some aspect that can be handled in 10 to 15 pages (about 2000 words).

Example

literature

↓

American literature

↓

Mark Twain

↓

Mark Twain's life as reflected in his writing

↓

Mark Twain and the Mississippi River

Note *how* these topics progress from a broad to a narrower aspect of the topic.

3. From library sources compile a bibliography of at least ten items on your narrowed subject. *At least three* items will represent current writing in periodicals. If you use books, indicate the chapters of the book that seem most pertinent.

4. Present your bibliography in proper form. Consult the Appendix, p. 259, for form.

▶ Exercise 2

1. Formulate a thesis for the paper on the narrowed topic you have chosen in Exercise 1. This will probably result in your taking a point of view toward your topic, and thus will narrow it still further.

Example

Mark Twain's personal experiences on the Mississippi River exert a controlling influence on his writing.

2. Write a paragraph or two of introduction to the paper. Begin with background material, perhaps giving reasons for discussing the topic or alternative points of view toward it. Then indicate the thesis or central idea and possibly suggest the organizational pattern that the paper is to follow.

PASSAGE FOR STUDY

Mark Twain and the Mississippi

Mark Twain's success as a writer has been attributed by some people to his skill in use of language—his gift for apt understatement, his ability to recount a tale in the words and rhythms of actual men and women. These are qualities of his style, and may have been developed through his encounters with people in Nevada and California mining camps or in San Francisco where, for some time, he was a newspaper reporter during the pioneer days. Undoubtedly the West influenced the style of the writing of the impressionable, observant Mark Twain. A more pervasive influence in his themes and subject matter, however, was the Mississippi River. The young Sam Clemens spent his boyhood in Hannibal, Missouri, where the arrival of the river steamer always brought life to the sleepy little town and afforded an escape from the petty problems of everyday living. The boats and the river had a special fascination for the boy. Thus, in his early adult life he became a pilot on the Mississippi, and his pen name, Mark Twain, is taken from river-pilot terminology. His writing reflects more than a mastery of style, however. The river developed within him certain perceptions, certain attitudes that form the theses of his novels.

The influence of the river is apparent in Twain's two best-known novels, *Tom Sawyer* and *Huckleberry Finn*. The Mississippi forms the background for *Tom Sawyer*. The adventures of Tom and Becky and of Injun Joe take place along the river and in caves on its bank. But in *Huckleberry Finn,* often considered Mark Twain's greatest work, the river is central. The problems and hazards that Huck and Jim experience in making their escape by boat and raft are drawn from the author's experience as a river pilot. His love for the river that came from his close association with it may be felt in the idyllic descriptions as Jim and Huck float along it under the stars. The river represents a place of refuge, of escape from the wickedness and corruption of men on shore. It becomes symbolic.

3. Answer the following questions about the example introduction you have just read:

a. What sentences indicate the central thesis of the paper?
b. In what way does the material that precedes the statement of the thesis prepare the reader for that statement?
c. How many parts might you expect the body of the paper to be divided into? What will they probably be?

4. Answer the same questions about the introduction that you write for this assignment. Note that the final limiting of the subject and statement of the thesis generally take place after the reading is done and the student sits down with his notes to plan how he will actually write the paper.

Extracting Pertinent Material
and Taking Notes on It

Three major things to remember in note taking are: (1) Do not take too many notes. (2) Sort out separate pieces of information that may go into different parts of your paper. (3) Take notes in your own words. This last problem is the greatest. If you take notes in the words of the author, these words tend to be transferred to the finished paper. The paper, then, is not wholly your own. These suggestions may aid you:

1. Read the sections of your source books and articles that you have decided may be pertinent to your purpose. Then *take notes after you have finished reading.* If you take notes as you read the first time, you may not be selective as to what you take notes on, and you waste time copying down material you may never use.

2. *Take notes in brief form.* You may want to outline a passage, following the author's line of thinking, or summarize an example or illustration. Summarizing is essentially a matter of removing redundancies, as you can see from the notes in Exercise 3, which follows.

3. Take your notes on cards, or small sheets of paper, putting *one fact, one quotation,* or *summary of one point on a card.* Later as you organize your paper, you can arrange your notes according to the section of the paper where you can best use the material.

4. Your *organizational pattern* may be clear in your mind before you gather your material, or it may become clear as you find material related to your subject and decide how best it can be put together. As you work out your pattern, sort your notes and *label each card* or slip of paper *according to the section of the paper where the material* on it *best fits.*

5. On each note card *make a notation indicating the source* of the material. This is particularly important, as you will want to footnote much of the material gained from your reading, and you will need all information, including page numbers, in the source. You may want to make the reference on the note card brief, if the complete reference is indicated in your bibliography, and may be referred to for footnoting.

6. If you are copying a passage that you expect to quote, write

down the material *exactly* as the author wrote it, and *put quotation marks around it.*

▶ **Exercise 3**

Assume you are writing a paper on language as a reflection of culture. As part of your reading you have included "How Different Cultures View Time," Lesson 3, p. 29, and "Rhetoric Across Cultures," Lesson 11, p. 108. Decide which of the three sets of notes that follow is the most suitable. Be prepared to comment on the strengths and weaknesses of each set and to defend your choice. Consider the following:

1. Has pertinent material been selected?
2. Is the material in brief form that is easily understandable?
3. Is it in the words of the writer of the paper rather than the words of the source?
4. If words of the source are used, are they presented in quotation marks?
5. Is the material labeled by topic so that it could easily be classified into a proper section of your paper?
6. Is the source for each fact given in enough detail so that you could identify the complete reference in the bibliography that you have prepared, and footnote properly?

Set 1

TIME AND CULTURE

Western European thought

   Past—behind us

   Future—in front of us

Quechua Indians—Peru

   Future—behind us because we cannot see it
   Past—in front because we can see it in our minds

Eugene Nida, *Customs and Culture,*
Reported in Ross and Doty, *WE,* pp. 29, 30.

REASONING AND CULTURE

Reasoning processes and procedures—same around the world

Inductive—generalizations based on examples

Deductive—major premise, minor an example of it

Premises differ in different cultures

Thus Lin Yutang comes to different conclusions when he reasons in Chinese and when he reasons in English.

"Rhetoric Across Cultures"
Ross and Doty, p. 109.

RHETORIC AND CULTURE

Introductions

English—comes to point quickly. States it in first paragraph.

Arrangement

Japanese—circles subject
Arab—restates

"Rhetoric Across Cultures"
Ross and Doty, p. 110.

Set 2

TIME

European culture—we "look back on" an event in the past. We say that events in the past are behind us. Similarly, we look forward to the future. The future is before us. For the Quechua Indians of Peru and Bolivia, however, the situation is different. They speak of the future as "behind oneself" and the past as ahead. They argue, "If you can think of the past and the future, which can you see with your mind's eye?" The obvious answer is that we can see the past and not the future, to which the Quechua replies, "Then if you can see the past, it must be ahead of you, and the future, which you cannot see, is behind you."

Ross and Doty, pp. 29, 30.

RHETORIC AND CULTURE

There are differences in rhetoric in cultures.

In introductions, speakers and writers of English are expected to come to the point as quickly as possible. It should be stated in the first paragraph.

In arrangement of ideas, the Japanese mentally circles the subject. The Arab loves restatement.

"Rhetoric Across Cultures"
Ross and Doty, p. 110.

Set 3

TIME

Not all cultures view time in the same way or mark the same time distinctions in their speech. Confusion exists in English because what we call present tense does not necessarily indicate present moment.

There is more than one valid way of viewing the same thing.

Ross and Doty, pp. 29, 30.

REASONING

All cultures engage in inductive and deductive reasoning

They have different premises. Lin Yutang thinks differently in Chinese and English.

Ross and Doty, p. 109.

RHETORIC

"To both the Japanese and the Arab student, English rhetoric, with its clear statement of purpose and economy of expression, will constitute a radical change in writing style."

Ross and Doty, p. 110.

► **Exercise 4**

For the paper on language as a reflection of culture proposed in Exercise 3, take notes on the selection "Language and Culture," Lesson 7, pp. 76, 77. Compare your notes with those of your classmates. Discuss them in relation to the check list in Exercise 3.

► **Exercise 5**

Find in the library another article or chapter from a book on language and culture. Take notes on it. Exchange notes with your classmates, and discuss the usefulness of the notes for a paper on language as a reflection of culture.

► **Exercise 6**

On the basis of the notes collected in Exercises 3, 4, and 5, which of the following do you think would make the most defensible thesis of a paper on language and culture? Be prepared to defend your choice.

1. Language determines the way in which one thinks.
2. Language reflects thought.
3. Cultural differences are reflected in language.
4. Culture determines language.

If you think none of these is appropriate, formulate a thesis of your own.

Integrating Material from Your Reading into a Composition of Your Own

Integrating material that you have read into a composition you write is one of the most difficult problems in writing a library paper, especially for students who do not feel completely at home in the language in which they are writing. The tendency is to copy large pieces of material word for word from the source, because since a native speaker of English presumably wrote it, his English must be correct. If you do this, however, *you* have not written the essay; the author of your source has written part of it for you. Moreover, you may be guilty of plagiarism—that is, presenting the work of someone else as though it were your own. Any extensive amount of plagiarism is an offense punishable by law. Many college professors watch for plagiarism, and they will give a failing grade to the writer of a paper containing large portions of material that the student has not formulated himself or put in the form of quotations with credit to the sources.

How, then, can you use facts, figures, explanations, summaries, examples, illustrations from your reading in a legitimate way, integrating them into a composition that you can present as your own? Here are some guiding principles:

1. Your paper should be your own in its *purpose,* its *organization,* and the *collection of material* it presents.

Your *purpose* should be your own. You have taken a point of view toward your subject, either before you begin to look for material, or in the process of gathering it. It reflects what *you,* not the author of one of your sources, plan to present. A helpful suggestion may be to turn your topic into a question; then read to find the answer. Your paper is your presentation of the answer.

Your *organizational plan* for fulfilling your purpose is your own. Because you are not following exactly what any one person said in any one selection that you have read, your main points will not be exactly the same as those of any other writer on the subject.

Your *material*—facts, figures, illustrations, and so on—will be gathered from various sources, not just from one. If it comes from only one source, you have merely given a summary of what one person said, and this rarely fulfills an assignment to "find out all you can about a subject and report on it," which is what is expected in most term papers. Your *collection of material* and the way in which it is presented must be your own.

2. In using material taken from your reading, *do not use the words of someone else without quoting, do not paraphrase long passages* without indicating clearly that you are doing so, and

do not merely piece together a series of paraphrases from a number of sources.

It is *legitimate to use the words of another person* if he has said what you want to say better than you can say it, or if you want to report his opinion or viewpoint *exactly as he presented it. Use quotation marks* and a *footnote.* Introduce your quotation by words such as "Ross and Doty say, ' . . . ' "

There are occasions on which *you may wish to paraphrase*— that is, to report what someone else said, but in your own words. If you want to report someone else's ideas or report work someone else has done *to support an idea of* your own, *precede the paraphrase by words indicating what you are doing.* Even more than with quotations, it is important to say in the body of your paper, for instance, "(author) reports that. . . ." or other similar expression, followed by your own words. *Use a footnote* to give the exact source.

Since your paper is your own, it should be written in your own words. If you try to put together notes from various sources in words close to those used in the source, the paper will not fit together well. Also, as indicated in the preceding paragraph, credit should be given for paraphrased passages.

3. To have a smoothly written paper which is your own, yet which presents ideas and material taken from other authors, it is often advisable to reread your notes, determine what you want to say, then *write your paper with as little reference as possible to your notes,* except to verify a fact, or introduce material that you wish to quote. You have read on your subject, have mastered it, and are now an "authority" on it in a minor way. You can put what you have gained from your reading with what you already knew about the subject, possibly from first-hand experience, or perhaps from earlier reading. What you have just read and what you already knew become blended.

▶ **Exercise 7**

The selection "An Unusual Bequest," Lesson 6, p. 65, was based on reading several sources, some of which gave the same information, and on personal recollections of visits to the Smithsonian Institution. Following are the notes for it that were taken from reading. They are presented in the order in which they were taken. Headings were added later to classify the material for ease in organizing the essay. Such headings are more important in a long paper than in a composition of this length.

Read the selection and study the notes. Then discuss with your classmates the answers to the questions on the sources and use of material in the final composition. Note that facts duplicating those noted in a previously read source are not given in notes. Places where information may be found are given.

Notes

1. (*Life,* Vol. 59, Nov. 19, 1965, pp. 86–98)

   Founder

   James Smithson. Illegitimate son of English nobleman.
   Died 1928. Denied title at home. Gave money to
   United States—a country he had never visited—
   to found organization with his name.

   Founding

   Objection of John C. Calhoun to receiving money
   from an Englishman, especially an illegitimate one!
   Declared: "It is beneath the dignity of the United States
   to accept presents of this kind."
   Congress grudgingly accepted.
   1838—clipper ship *Mediator*—sailed to N.Y. with 105
   bags of gold sovereigns. Coins sent to Phila., melted
   down and cast into American coins. Value $508,318.46.
   Scientific aspect originally emphasized. First secretary—
   Joseph Henry—one of the developers of the
   electromagnet.

   Size and Value

   Largest museum in the world.
   7 buildings. Zoo at Rock Creek Park. Renwick house—
   recently opened. Value more than a billion dollars.

   Collections

   Called nation's attic.
   Largest collection of flags in the world.
   Inaugural gowns of president's wives.
   Hall of Transportation—warship from American Revolution.
   Lindbergh's plane. First spaceship to go to the moon.

One locomotive so big building had to be constructed
around it. Automobiles—history of motor car.

Items belonging to presidents—Washington's sword,
shoes made for Jefferson by slave, Eisenhower's uniform,
Wilson's cane, Hoover's fishing rod.

2. (Smithsonian pamphlet)

Collections

Only half a million items—less than 1 percent of total—
on display.

Largest museum in the world.

Collection given from Phila. exhibition—won it title—
"nation's attic."

Activities

18 million visitors a year.

Over 300 scientists—research.

3. (Leonard Carmichael and J. C. Long, *James Smithson and
the Smithsonian Story,* G. P. Putnam's Sons, 1965)

Founder

James Smithson, one of four illegitimate children of Duke
of Northumberland.

Grew up in France under mother's name of Macy. Mother
left England, destroyed all records to avoid scandal.
Smithson returns to England as young man. Takes
father's name—Smithson. No title.

Impressed by work of British Royal Institution, organization to make knowledge, especially in field of science,
available to people. Stated in will money used "to found
at Washington under the name of the Smithsonian Institution an establishment for the increase and diffusion of
knowledge."

Activities and Collections (Detailed information with
pictures)

Solar radiation. Home planning.

Questions

1. Indicate whether the source of each of the following statements
taken from the finished composition "An Unusual Bequest" is
probably (a) a comment of the writer of the selection, (b) a

comment of one of the authors of the sources used in the composition (this would need footnoting and possibly quotation marks), (c) a fact taken from reading, or (d) a fact based on personal observation.

a. The Smithsonian Institution in Washington, D.C., is the largest museum in the world.

b. The Smithsonian is an unusual institution, not only in the extent of its collections and the activities it carries on, but also in the manner of its founding.

c. Many of the displays reflect the growth and development of the country.

d. The transportation exhibit includes a warship dating from the time of the American Revolution as well as the first spaceship to go to the moon.

e. One locomotive engine in the collection is so large that the building had to be constructed around it.

f. In the display of objects associated with presidents one may see the uniform worn by President Eisenhower when he was a general in the U.S. Army.

g. The National Gallery of Art, containing priceless paintings from all over the world, is part of the Smithsonian.

h. The origin of the Smithsonian Institution is perhaps more unusual than the extent of its collection and the range of its activities.

i. Congress grudgingly accepted the gift.

j. The results of their work are reported in the Smithsonian's many publications.

2. Find three examples of material in the notes that were not used in the selection.

3. Find at least one example of material in the selection that was not in the notes.

Giving Proper Credit to Your Sources

Giving proper credit to your sources has been discussed in part in the preceding section. In general one should footnote:

1. Direct quotations
2. Paraphrases
3. Little-known facts, or facts that someone might possibly question

The footnoting of quotations and paraphrases has already been discussed. The footnoting of facts is not quite as clear-cut. Are they relatively unknown? Might the reader want to verify them? Do you want the authority of the source in which you found them to support you in your use of them?

You might study the use of footnoting in this book. Passages for study that have been taken word for word from another source are footnoted. Others might say, "Adapted from (name of author and source)." In writing some of the passages for study in Part I, the authors in some cases relied on published sources for the facts, but the passages were rewritten to illustrate grammatical principles. When the passage is based on one source, it is footnoted to indicate the source. Note the passages "Adventure on the Colorado" and "Undersea Museums." When a passage is based on general reading or on first-hand observation (the passage "Mesa Verde" is an example), no footnoting is used.

Note that in writing a research paper the author of that paper has sole responsibility for the format of the acknowledgments in the footnotes and the bibliography. Since this is so, the format of these acknowledgments should be consistent. The correct form for footnotes and bibliography is indicated on pp. 258–259 of the Appendix. You may wish to follow, instead, one of the common form sheets, such as the Modern Language Association style sheet. There are variations in recommended forms. The authors of commercial writing, such as textbooks, must follow the format prescribed by the holder of the copyright; therefore, since copyright holders differ in the format they approve, the form of footnotes in such books is often inconsistent.

You may run into other problems in writing term papers and theses. The point in the preparation process at which you can finally limit your topic and state it specifically is difficult to determine because it depends in part on the material that you are able to find. Determining the organizational pattern is also affected by this. The four points covered in this lesson, however, are those that are peculiar to writing papers based on reading, and are those that seem to cause the greatest problems for native users of the language, and perhaps even greater ones for those studying English as a foreign language.

A final word: Do not quote and do not paraphrase unless you give your source. An entire paper should not be made of paraphrases and quotations.

▶ **Exercise 8**

Little-known facts *taken from one specific source* are footnoted so that they can be verified. Footnoting relieves the writer of responsibility for information that he has not acquired at first hand. Be able to explain why the statements in Exercise 7, p. 216, taken from "An Unusual Bequest" were not footnoted when they were used in the selection in Lesson 6.

▶ **Exercise 9**

The following selection is an example of the way researchers should use material gathered from reading. Although the views of many people are quoted, the overall discussion is the product of the editors. This selection constitutes two sections of a *Time* cover story entitled "In Quest of Leadership." In these sections the writers try to define what leadership is and they discuss whether leadership can be taught. Read the selection and answer the questions that follow it.

PASSAGE FOR STUDY

For and Against Heroes[1]

(1) And no one of course is sure just what leadership is. Historians and others who have thought about it cite innumerable

---

[1] Lance Morrow, Janice Castro, and Gay McIntosh, "In Quest of Leadership," *Time,* July 15, 1974, 23, 24, 28. Reprinted by permission from *Time,* The Weekly Newsmagazine; Copyright Time Inc.

definitions and distinctions involving politics and war, moral force and intellectual power, good and evil. . . . Among the most lucid and sweeping definitions is this one, proposed by the French critic Henri Peyre: "Leadership can be but a broad ideal proposed by the culture of a country, instilled into the young through the schools, but also through the family, the intellectual atmosphere, the literature, the history, the ethical teaching of that country. Will power, sensitivity to the age, clear thinking rather than profound thinking, the ability to experience the emotions of a group and to voice their aspirations, joined with control over those emotions in oneself, a sense of the dramatic . . . are among the ingredients of the power to lead men."

(2) Most definitions emphasize honesty, candor and vision combined with sheer physical stamina and courage. Not that courage without brains was ever sufficient. An episode from British history emphasizes the point. When the British Cabinet summoned the Duke of Wellington and asked him who was the ablest general to take Rangoon, the unhesitating reply was "Lord Combermere." "But we have always understood that your Grace thought Lord Combermere a fool," the Cabinet protested. "So he is a fool, and a damned fool," said Wellington. "But he can take Rangoon."

(3) What of that mysterious quality called charisma? "It would be nice to have charisma," says M.I.T. President Jerome Weisner. "But you would like it to be based on an understanding of what the hell is going on." (Weisner adds that anyone who claims to understand all the issues is a fraud.) Forget charisma, suggests Columbia University Historian Richard Morris. "Do we really need the charismatic, individualistic leadership that the nation boasted in its infancy?" he wonders. "Perhaps our century has had a surfeit of charismatic figures. Today we could do with honest ones." Like many other historians, Morris seems to perceive two starkly contrasting types of leadership—the charismatic *v.* the more or less commonplace. More often the two poles are defined as the romantic and the functional.

(4) It was Thomas Carlyle who articulated the beginning of the modern romantic cycle. "The history of the world," he wrote in 1841, "is but the biography of great men." Hitler elaborated the argument with Hegel's theory of the "world-historical figure"—the heroic genius who emerges when the historical moment is right to lead a people to their preordained destiny.

(5) That thought merged a kind of messianism with Hegelian and Marxian determinism, the idea that vast and blind historical

forces sweep across the world's stage without important regard to personalities. But of course that Marxist thought is invalidated by Marxist history—the crucial "heroic" role played by men like Marx himself, and Lenin and Stalin. Arthur Schlesinger Jr. suggests that "men have lived who did what no substitute could ever have done; their intervention set history on one path rather than another. If this is so, the old maxim 'There are no indispensable men' would seem another amiable fallacy. There is, then, a case for heroes."

(6) Henry Kissinger does not deny that this case can be made, but he worries about the damage that such towering figures can cause. "Institutions are designed for an average standard of performance—a high average in fortunate societies, but still a standard reducible to approximate norms," Kissinger wrote . . . in an essay on Bismarck. "They are rarely able to accommodate genius or demoniac power. A society that must produce a great man in each generation to maintain its domestic or international position will doom itself."

Can Leadership Be Taught?

(7) Such exceptional figures remain one of the enigmas of civilization. Leaders, wrote Peyre, "are indeed mystery men born in paradise or some devil's pit." In his brilliant study of Gandhi, Erik Erikson detected a "shrewdness [that] seemed to join his capacity to focus on the infinite meaning in finite things—a trait which is often associated with the attribution of sainthood." The rule that great leaders are summoned forth by great issues can be persuasively argued from, say, the Churchillian example—a brilliant, irascible aristocrat who was settling into a relatively unsuccessful old age when the war called him forth to embody a people's grand defiance.

(8) Another example is Charles de Gaulle, who lived through his country's defeat and waited through political exile before he re-emerged and then managed through a combination of shrewdness, style and, indeed, charisma to act on the world stage as if France were still a great power. But he also had the courage to ignore passion and face reality in Algeria, cutting his country's losses in a disastrous colonial war.

(9) In the U.S. perhaps only Lincoln and Franklin Roosevelt played comparable roles in profound crises that threatened the very survival of the society. But the phenomenon is wholly unpredictable; there have been numerous upheavals in human history—the medieval plagues in Europe, for example—in which the event did

not summon a savior. Ireland's eternal troubles illustrate history's frequent refusal to beckon a great leader with a solution. At the same time, great leaders throughout history have arisen seemingly from nowhere, like the Mahdi, an Islamic mystic who drove the Egyptians and their British allies, led by General Charles Gordon, out of the Sudan in a 19th century holy war.

(10) Men have often dealt with the unpredictability of leadership by citing a hero's or prophet's appearance as divine intervention, since ordinary historical rules could not explain it. Thus Moses. Thus the emergence of Mohammed, whose startling religious and political career could scarcely have been predicted at the time.

(11) The darker side of the thesis that great issues summon great men is the fact that great issues often mean simply great confusion, and that chaos can just as well call forth monsters. Psychiatrists D. Wilfred Abse and Lucie Jessner believe that "in its most extreme form, the leader-follower relationship exists in the rapport of hypnotist and subject." . . .

(12) In the U.S., the balance between charismatic and pragmatic leadership has usually been weighted toward the latter. The earliest American concept of leadership was really neither; it had its roots in the Age of Reason and Greek political philosophy. Plato's intention was to make the joys and sorrows of every citizen the joys and sorrows of all. The individual was an integrated part of the whole social body striving for excellence. The ideal was total *noblesse oblige,* an excellence of virtue based on justice, or *paideia.* Something of that ideal informed Jefferson's notion of the *aristoi*—the natural aristocracy based on virtue and talents whose members were the best governors for society. It survives in the deepest roots of the American establishment, even though the aristocratic tendency runs counter to Jacksonian exuberance, the more egalitarian American strain that makes every man a king.

(13) Whether aristocratic or egalitarian in concept, can leadership be taught? It is one of the more tantalizing questions at a time when the quality is seen to be in such short supply. The military has often proved an effective, if not the only, school for leadership—consider Alexander, Genghis Khan, Napoleon. The late Harvard sociologist Pitirim Sorokin has documented the stunning extent to which the military has been the route to power for men of humble origins. "Of 92 Roman Emperors," Sorokin wrote, "at least 36 climbed to this position from the lowest social strata up the army ladder; of 65 Emperors of Byzantium, at least 12 were really upstarts who obtained this position through the same army

ladder." In the U.S. a military career has rarely led to wider leadership in this century except in the very special case of Dwight Eisenhower.

(14) Various societies have set about schooling their young for leadership. It is an ambiguous enterprise. Four of the nine British public schools known as the Clarendon Schools (Eton, Harrow, Winchester and Rugby) have produced a disproportionate number of leaders over the years. Someone who passed through the system wrote: "It was assumed that every boy would be in such position as Viceroy of India and must be brought up with this end in view. The government of the country was made an almost personal matter." So too with Oxford and Cambridge, which have produced British leaders for centuries. At work there was a deep tradition of elitism and stability, a continuity of assumptions and expectations.

(15) But the English aristocracy was capable of disastrous follies. There is no more perfect indictment of such leadership than the fatuously self-confident direction by the Lords Raglan and Cardigan of the charge of the Light Brigade. The event must be seen in retrospect not just as a piece of heroic military stupidity (worse ones have occurred since), but as a symbol of what happens to a trained elite that is closed to new blood and new ideas.

(16) In the U.S. perhaps the most important form of leadership training has been the legal profession. However one may feel about lawyers, their predominance among U.S. political leaders suggests a deep American desire to mediate between opposing passions.

(17) But Americans have had little patience with formal leadership training outside the military academies and some business-management courses, where the emphasis is often on case studies and field work. "Leadership can be developed and improved by study and training," General Omar Bradley once told a class at the Army Command and General Staff College in Fort Leavenworth, Kans. "But don't discount experience. Someone may remind you that Napoleon led armies before he was 30 and Alexander the Great died at 33. Alexander might have been even greater if he had lived to an older age and had had more experience. In this respect, I especially like [the] theory that 'judgment comes from experience and experience comes from bad judgment.'" . . .

(18) Alexis de Tocqueville foresaw that democracy would have the effect of flattening the peaks of excellence while elevating the sub-par or the average. The danger is that in glorifying the least common denominator, democracy mandates mediocrity. The hope

is that such a system will encourage a universal standard of excellence in every pursuit. Tocqueville took it for granted that the leveling process in a democracy would produce a mean—but not a happy mean. Nonetheless, democracy possesses a resilience and fluidity that are capable of defying such predictions: classes rise above themselves, ambition remains plausible. Indeed, Americans hardly realize how revolutionary—and vulnerable—is the idea that a nation can have leadership without a trained elite, a leadership subject to popular mandate.

(19) There is widespread fear today of new "men on horseback," of new demagogues. As governments wrestle with the problem of distributing ever more limited resources, thinkers like U.S. Economist Robert Heilbroner foresee a Hobbesian descent into authoritarianism and a siege economy in many nations—even in America. Heilbroner believes that perhaps modern man's aggressive and competitive instincts can be transferred from nature-destroying production to services—education, health care and the arts. But he doubts this can be done without paying a "fearful price" in democratic freedoms.

Questions

1. Sentence 2 in paragraph 1 of the preceding selection indicates the breadth of research the authors have done. It forces the reader to ask questions such as these:
   a. Should a man whose life is devoted to evil (such as a leading gangster) be called a great leader?
   b. If so, what qualities that he possesses are similar to qualities in the "good" leader?
   c. Is leadership, then, a thing apart from morals?
   d. Is it also apart from intellect?
   What questions does sentence 2 make *you* ask?
2. The assertions made in this selection are supported largely by quotation from authority. What other form of support is used in paragraph 2?
3. Restate in formal language the idea expressed in the quotation from Jerome Weisner in paragraph 3. What does the style of Weisner's language add to this discussion?

4. Why do the authors restate Morris' point in the last two sentences of paragraph 3?

5. Be prepared to discuss the train of thought in paragraphs 3, 4, and 5. How do the authors disagree with Hegel and Marx? In which sentence?

6. In what way do Arthur Schlesinger, Jr., and Henry Kissinger disagree about heroes? What word serves to tie paragraph 6 to paragraph 5?

7. In a paragraph summarize as briefly as possible the points made in the selection "For and Against Heroes."

8. Is the purpose of the article to mold public opinion or to stimulate thought? Give reasons for your answer.

9. Discuss the differences between the British and the American philosophy of training leaders, touching on the advantages and dangers in each method. (This discussion may be written or may be done orally in class.)

10. This material contains no footnotes telling the names of the books from which the quotations have been taken. Can you surmise the reason?

11. In paragraph 7 is there any connection between the quotation from Erik Erikson and the example of Churchill? State the connection in one sentence. Have the authors stated the connection? Explain.

12. Would "How Are Leaders Produced?" be a better title for this selection? Discuss why or why not.

13. In paragraphs 7 through 11, the authors discuss whether crises produce leaders. Do the authors give all the evidence on one side and then all the evidence on the other? Discuss the patterning (or organization) of the material here and to what extent it is effective.

14. What kind of supporting material is used in paragraph 13? Has this type been used earlier in this passage? If, as a leader of a country, you were contemplating the establishment of a school to train leaders, what other figures might you want to examine before you made your decision?

15. Reread this passage, underlining the words of the authors. (Do not underline the quotations or paraphrases of other people's ideas.) Study this underlined material, and the role of an author of a research article will become apparent.

Composition

Write on one of the following.

A. If it is required for another course, write the paper that you planned in Exercise 1 and 2 in this lesson. Pay particular attention to footnoting. Include the bibliography.

B. Write a paper on the relationship between language and culture based on notes and reading, for Exercises 3, 4, 5, and 6. After notes have been checked you may wish to exchange notes and information with other members of the class. Pay particular attention to footnoting. Include a bibliography.

Appendix

I. Charts of Selected Grammatical Points

A. *Nouns*

1. IRREGULAR PLURALS OF NOUNS

General rules

Plurals of nouns are regularly formed by adding -*s* or -*es*. Most nouns add -*s* (*hat–hats, boy–boys*). Nouns ending in -*s*, -*x*, -*z* and -*sh* add -*es* (*dish–dishes, dress–dresses, porch–porches, fox–foxes*). Some nouns ending in -*o* preceded by a consonant and -*es*.

echo–echoes	veto–vetoes	tornado–tornadoes
potato–potatoes	tomato–tomatoes	hero–heroes
Exceptions: piano–pianos		soprano–sopranos
solo–solos		Filipino–Filipinos

Nouns ending in -*y* preceded by a consonant change the -*y* to -*i* and add -*es*.

city–cities	baby–babies
lady–ladies	body–bodies

Some nouns ending in -*f* change the -*f* to -*v* and add -*es*.

leaf–leaves	half–halves	knife–knives
life–lives	shelf–shelves	loaf–loaves
Exceptions: proof–proofs	grief–griefs	gulf–gulfs
roof–roofs	belief–beliefs	safe–safes

Some nouns ending in -*f* have two plurals.

elf–elfs, elves	wharf–wharfs, wharves
hoof–hoofs, hooves	scarf–scarfs, scarves

Irregular old English plurals

Some irregular plurals that are survivals of Old English forms are:

child–children   man–men   foot–feet   goose–geese
ox–oxen   woman–women   tooth–teeth mouse–mice

Foreign plurals retained in English

Some foreign words (particularly Latin and Greek words) taken into English retain their foreign plurals. A few examples are:

analysis–   criterion–   phenomenon–
  analyses   criteria   phenomena
basis–bases   datum–data   radius–radii
crisis–crises   hypothesis–hypotheses   stratum–strata

Nouns with the same form for singular and plural
Nationalities: Chinese, Japanese, Swiss
Animals: deer, sheep, fish, trout, salmon, fowl

---

2. CLASSES OF NON-COUNT NOUNS[a]

Group I. Abstractions

beauty*	intelligence	permission*	abuse*
ugliness	stupidity	refusal*	assistance
blame	joy*	poverty	command*
praise*	sorrow*	wealth	contempt
bravery	laughter	strength*	deference
cowardice	weeping	weakness*	enjoyment
confidence*	love*	tragedy*	faith*
timidity	hate*	comedy*	gaiety*
death*	luck	trouble*	isolation
life*	misfortune*	fortune*	justice*
health	nonsense	victory*	kindness*
sickness*	sense*	defeat*	neglect
ignorance	patience	virtue*	opportunity*
knowledge	impatience	vice*	power*
infancy	peace	youth*	right*
old age	war*	maturity	work*

Group II. Substances

	Food			Nonfood		
Solids		**Liquids**	**Solids**		**Liquids**	**Gases**
bacon	yogurt	cream	coal	silver	gasoline	air
beef	celery	soup*	sand*	lead	oil	
sausage*	cabbage*	water*	cement	tin*		
pork	grapefruit*	milk	iron*	hair*		
ham*	pineapple*	oil*	steel	cotton*		
lamb	corn*	vinegar*	dirt	fur*		
chicken*	sugar	tea	soot	linen*		
fish*	rice	coffee	dust	silk*		
bread*	flour*		gold	wool*		
butter	coffee					
cheese*	salt					
ice cream	pepper					
jelly*						

Group III. Collections

	Inanimate (nonliving)		Animate (living)
architecture	information	news	humanity
clothing	jewelry	postage	man
entertainment	luggage	recreation	mankind
equipment	lumber	scenery	personnel
fruit*	lumber	traffic	woman
furniture	merchandise	transportation	youth
hardware	money	weather	

Group IV. Phenomena and forces of nature

cold	fog*	mist*	sound*
daylight	gravity	moonlight	sunlight
darkness	hail	rain*	thunder*
electricity	heat	smoke*	water*
fire*	lightning	snow*	wind*

Group V. Areas of study and activity

agriculture	fun	art*	hiking	football
business*	leisure	chemistry	reading	hockey
commerce	play*	economics	shopping	soccer
farming	work*	linguistics	swimming	tennis
science*		literature*	writing*	
		music	(most nouns	
		philosophy*	with –ing)	
		physics		
		Spanish		
		statistics		

ᵃ Nouns marked with an asterisk (*) are also frequently used as count nouns. Compare: *Joy* is better than sorrow. Do you know *the joys* of raising a large family? When used as count nouns, these nouns sometimes have slightly different meanings.

B. *Verbs*

1. Irregular Verbs

Present	Past	Past participle	Present	Past	Past participle
am (is)	was	been	fly	flew	flown
arise	arose	arisen	forget	forgot	forgot,
awake	awoke	awakened			forgotten
bear	bore	borne	freeze	froze	frozen
beat	beat	beat(en)	get	got	got, gotten
become	became	become	give	gave	given
begin	began	begun	go	went	gone
bend	bent	bent	grow	grew	grown
bet	bet	bet	hang	hanged	hanged
bid	bade	bidden			(execute)
bid	bid	bid	hang	hung	hung
bite	bit	bitten	have	had	had
bleed	bled	bled	hear	heard	heard
blow	blew	blown	hide	hid	hidden
bring	brought	brought	hit	hit	hit
build	built	built	hold	held	held
burst	burst	burst	hurt	hurt	hurt
buy	bought	bought	keep	kept	kept
catch	caught	caught	know	knew	known
choose	chose	chosen	lay	laid	laid
come	came	come	lead	led	led

Present	Past	Past participle	Present	Past	Past participle
cost	cost	cost	leave	left	left
creep	crept	crept	lend	lent	lent
cut	cut	cut	let	let	let
deal	dealt	dealt	lie	lay	lain
dig	dug	dug	lie	lied	lied (tell an
dive	dived	dived			untruth
do	did	done	light	lighted, lit	lighted, lit
draw	drew	drawn	lose	lost	lost
drink	drank	drunk	make	made	made
drive	drove	driven	mean	meant	meant
eat	ate	eaten	meet	met	met
fall	fell	fallen	pay	paid	paid
feel	felt	felt	put	put	put
fight	fought	fought	quit	quit	quit
find	found	found	read	read	read
rid	rid	rid	sting	stung	stung
ride	rode	ridden	strike	struck	struck
ring	rang	rung	stick	stuck	stuck
rise	rose	risen	swear	swore	sworn
run	ran	run	sweep	swept	swept
say	said	said	swim	swam	swum
see	saw	seen	swing	swung	swung
sell	sold	sold	take	took	taken
send	sent	sent	teach	taught	taught
set	set	set	tear	tore	torn
shake	shook	shaken	tell	told	told
shine	shone	shone	think	thought	thought
shoot	shot	shot	throw	threw	thrown
shrink	shrank	shrunk	understand	understood	understood
shut	shut	shut	upset	upset	upset
sing	sang	sung	wake	waked,	waked,
sink	sank	sunk		woke	wakened
sit	sat	sat	wear	wore	worn
sleep	slept	slept	weave	wove	woven
slide	slid	slid	wed	wed	wed
speak	spoke	spoken	weep	wept	wept
spend	spent	spent	wet	wet, wetted	wet, wetted
spread	spread	spread	win	won	won
spring	sprang	sprung	wind	wound	wound
stand	stood	stood	wring	wrung	wrung
steal	stole	stolen	write	wrote	written

2. Verbs Followed by Verbals

Verbs followed directly by infinitive (*to* + verb) as complement

ask	desire	go[a]	plan
be	dislike	hate	prefer
beg	dread	hope	promise
begin	endeavor	intend	remember
care	expect	learn	try
cease	forget	like	start
continue	get (be allowed,	mean	stop
decide	become)	neglect	want
			wish

Example

We wanted *to go.*

Verbs followed by noun or pronoun + infinitive as complement

advise	encourage	oblige	tell
allow	expect	order	urge
ask	force	persuade	want
beg	get (persuade)	prefer	warn
cause	instruct	promise	wish
command	invite	remind	
desire		teach	

Example

We invited *him to accompany* us.

Verbs followed by v + *–ing* as complement

admit	deny	intend	practice	start
allow	dislike	keep	prefer	stop
appreciate	dread	keep on	put off	talk over
avoid	enjoy	like	quit	talk over
begin	escape	miss	remember	try
be worth	finish	neglect	resent	
cease	hate	plan	resist	
consider	imagine	postpone	risk	
continue				

Examples

He dislikes *traveling.*
He denied *being* there yesterday.

[a] *Going* + an infinitive expresses the future intent: I am *going to do* it.

Verbs followed by noun or pronoun + simple verb

feel	hear	let	see
have	help	make	watch

Examples

I heard *him leave* this morning.
I will have *my sister go* with me.

Verbs followed by noun or pronoun + v–*ed, –en*

consider	have	keep	order
feel	hear	imagine	want

Examples

He will *get it done* tomorrow.
I *consider the subject closed.*

3. Patterns Containing Auxiliary Verbs

SUMMARY OF VERB PATTERNS EXPRESSING MODES

Group I. Modal auxiliaries

I will (would) go.
I can (could) come.
He may (might) agree with you.
I shall (should) do it.
We had better leave now.
They must leave immediately.
But: He ought *to* do it.

Group II. Other auxiliaries expressing modes

He has (had) *to* do it.
The class is (was) *to* have an examination tomorrow.
We are (were) going *to* tell you about it.
My friends are (were) about *to* leave for the United States.
The secretary gets (got) *to* award the prize

USES OF GROUP I. MODAL AUXILIARIES

Will + v

A. Future time

The English language has no inflectional form for the future tense as it does for the simple past. The use of *will* or *shall* is a common way of expressing the future.[a] *Will* also suggests willingness, or a promise or an agreement with another person's wishes, in addition to implying futurity.

We will meet you on the corner in twenty minutes.
The workmen will come tomorrow to repair the roof.
My secretary will call you tomorrow.
I will let you know as soon as the work is finished.

B. Requests

Will is used in making polite requests.

Will you please take this package to the post office for me?
Will you please be seated?

C. Questions about future matters

These questions do not concern advisability or make requests. (See *shall,* p. 240.)

Will we have many examinations in this course?
Will the meeting of the council take place tomorrow?

---

[a] The future is also expressed by other auxiliaries like *am about to* or *am going to* or by the present tense with an adverbial element denoting future time (*I go to New York tomorrow*), or by other modals with an adverbial element denoting future time (*I can go next week*). *I am going to* + verb stresses intention to do something. See p. 35.

Would + v

A. Willingness

The use of *would* here is similar to *will*.

I would (will) be glad to help you.

B. Desires

Would is used with *like* to express desire.

I would like a cup of coffee.
I would like to speak to you today about my country.

C. Conditional or hypothetical situations

Would is most commonly used to express desires or willingness in hypothetical situations.

I would do it if I knew how.
If you would do it for me, I would be very grateful.

D. Habitual action in the past

When I was a child I would often walk in the country.

E. Past tense of *will*

Would is used as the past tense of *will* in reported speech.

He says he will go.   (present)
He said he would go.   (past)

F. Polite requests

This use of *would* is similar to that of *will*.

Would you mind opening the door for me?

Can + v

A. Ability

Can expresses the ability to do something in the immediate present or in the future. In this sense it is the equivalent of *to be able to*.

I can speak five languages.   (present)
I can help you next week.   (future)

B. Permission

Can is used in statements implying permission as well as ability. *Can* in question asking permission is colloquial. (See *may*, p. 239.)

My secretary can help you this afternoon.
Can (may) I go with you?

Could + v

A. Ability

Could indicates ability to do something in the past. In this sense it is the past of *can*.

When I was six years old I could speak only one language; now I can speak five.

B. Conditional

Could expresses the ability to do something if other conditions are met. The past tense is expressed by *could have*.

I could buy a new car if I had the money.
I could have asked him if I had seen him.

C. Possibility

The use of *could* to express a possibility is much like its use to express a conditional situation.

I hear someone coming down the hall. It could be John.

D. Past tense of *can*

Could is the past tense of *can* in reported speech.

John says he can repair your typewriter. (present)
John said he could repair your typewriter. (past)

May + v

A. Permission

May is used to express permission or to indicate that something is allowed. Present or future time is indicated.

> You may go now. (You have permission to go immediately.)
> You may leave when you have finished the examination.
> (You have permission to leave at a future time.)
> Your name may be placed in the right-hand corner of your paper.

B. Questions asking permission

May is commonly used in questions asking permission. (See *can*, p. 238.)

> May I come in? (immediate action)
> May I come tomorrow? (future action)

C. Conjectures

May sometimes indicates conjecture about the future. When used in this sense, the past tense is indicated by *may have*.

> It may rain tomorrow. (There is a strong possibility.)
> It may have rained while we were gone. (The speaker is not sure whether it did or not.)

Might + v

A. Conjecture

Might expressing conjecture is sometimes used interchangeably with *may,* or it may have a stronger implication that the condition is hypothetical or contrary to fact. The past tense is expressed by *might have.* (Compare with the use of *may,* previously.)

> It might rain tomorrow.
> It might have rained while we were gone.
> I might build a new house if I had the money. (The situation is hypothetical or contrary to fact.)

B. Past tense of *may*

Might is used as the past tense of *may* in reported speech.

> John says that I may go with him. (present)
> John said that I might go with him. (past)

Shall + v

A. Questions of advisability in the first person

This is the main use of *shall*. *Shall* refers to the future.

Shall I close the window?
Shall we go to the play on Thursday night?

B. Future tense

Shall is sometimes used in the first person to express the future tense. The use of *will* is more common.

We shall know the answer to this problem tomorrow.

Should + v

A. Obligation

Should indicates obligation in regard to a general truth or to a specific act. It generally indicates an obligation which is recognized but which is not necessarily being fulfilled. In this sense it has a meaning close to that of *ought to*. Unfulfilled obligation in the past is expressed by *should have*.

We should be courteous to our parents. (obligation; a general truth)
I should mail this letter. (obligation regarding a specific act)
I should study tonight, but I am going to the movies. (obligation recognized but unfulfilled)
You should have answered the letters today.

B. Advisability

Should represents advisability as well as obligation.

You should have answered the letters today.
four-o'clock train.

C. Possibility

Should may also indicate a strong possibility that probably will be fulfilled.

I should get a letter from my insurance company today.

D. Questions of advisability in the first person

The use of *should* here is similar to that of *shall*. *Should* implies more of a sense of advisability than *shall*.

Should we close the windows before we leave?

Must + v

A. Necessity

This is the most common use of *must*.

People must eat in order to live.
Doctors must be concerned for their patients.
I must take the books back to the library; they are overdue.

Must expressing necessity has no past tense. Necessity in past time is expressed by *had to*.

B. Inference

Must indicates inference only with certain verbs the verb *have;* linking verbs like *seem, appear,* and *be;* verbs expressing desire like *want, need,* and *believe;* and certain verbs expressing physical activity such as *walk, run, drive,* and so forth.

There must be a lot of stamps in that drawer; I remember putting them there.
Mr. Briggs must have an early class at the university; I see him leaving the house every day at seven-thirty.
He must take the bus to work; I see him pass this corner every morning.

Inference in the past may be expressed by *must have.*

It must have rained here yesterday; there is a lot of water on the ground.
John must have won the prize. He looks very pleased.

Ought to + v

Ought to + v has much the same meaning as *should,* but note the contrast in form.

I should go downtown this afternoon.
I ought to go downtown this afternoon.
We should finish this today.
We ought to finish this today. (We expect to finish it or we have an obligation to finish it.)

Have to + v

Have to + v expresses necessity in much the same way that *must* + v does. *Have to* and *must* can be used interchangeably. However, note the contrast in form.

I must leave now.
You must pay your fees today.
I have to leave now.
You have to pay your fees today.

Necessity in the past time is expressed by *had to*.

I had to leave then.
We had to pay our fees yesterday.

However, different meanings are expressed by *must not* and *do not have to*. Compare these two sentences:

You must not drive 80 miles an hour; it is against the law. (It is necessary that you not do it.)
You do not have to drive so fast. We have plenty of time to get there. (It is not necessary that you do it.)

Am to + v, *Am Going to* + v, *Am About to* + v

Am to, am going to, and *am about to* are all ways of expressing the future. Note the differences in meaning signaled by these expressions.

I am going to visit my sister next week. (intention to act at some indefinite future time, perhaps next week)
I am about to leave. (within the next few minutes)
I am to give a talk for her club while I am there. (The members of the club expect me to do it. They have asked me to do it. I plan to do it.)
Albert was to have gone with me, but he cannot leave his business. (He expected to go. He planned to go.)
He was going to take me in his car, but now I am going to take the train. (He planned in the past to do it in the future.)

C. Prepositions

1. USES OF PREPOSITIONS IN ADVERBIAL PHRASES

Time

in: in the evening (morning)
in the fall (season)
in August (month)
in 1952 (year)
in two months (meaning
at the end of)
in time (idiom meaning
early enough)

for: I skied for an hour.

from: from Friday till
Monday from that
moment

to: He left at ten minutes to
two.

on: on August 12 (definite
date)
on Friday (day of the
week)
on Christmas (holiday)
on your birthday
(definite day)
on time (idiom meaning
punctual)

by: by eight o'clock (not
later than)
They worked by the
hour (were paid
hourly wages).

with: With the approach of
fall the air gets
cooler.

Place or direction

at: He is at the dentist's.
He looked at me.
He was angry at John.

of: It lies south of the
border.

on: He wanted a house on
the coast (river bank,
etc.).

from: They live miles from
here.
We went from
laughter to tears.

in: He lives in an apartment.
He lives in a dream.

to: The temperature
dropped to zero.
He went to the river.
He contributed to the
Red Cross.
This procedure is to
your advantage (idio-
matic expression).

with: He lived with the
Johnsons.
The outcome rests
with you.

Means or agent

by: The boat was built by an Italian.
He came by plane.
I did it by myself (without help).
It arrived by airmail.
By wrapping it yourself, you save money.

on: We saw it on television.
He is going on foot.
They live on meat.

from: His honors come from hard work.
She is burned from sunbathing.

with: He opened it with a knife.

Manner

in: In my estimation the act was noble.
His joy is in helping others.
He left in anger.
She was dressed in blue.
It appealed to us in several ways.

like: He looks like me.

on: I swear this on my honor.

with: He said it with a smile.

by: They work by the week.

State or condition

at: The nurses are at work.
The nations are at peace.
The soldiers stood at ease.
We are at your mercy.
He smiled at the thought

by: We were all by ourselves last night (without company).

on: The pharmacist is on call all night.

in: He was in a hurry.

Quantity

for: We drove for 50 miles.
The suit sold for $50.

to: He bet 4 to 1 on that horse.
Our team won the football game 14 to 7.

by: The mosquitoes arrived by the thousands.
The garden was 30 by 60 feet.
They are sold by the pair.

Purpose

for: He went for an education.
      He came for a rest.
      He was hired for his creativity.
      He asked for a vacation.
      This gift is for you.

Association or possession

to: It belongs to John.
    He is faithful to his be-
      liefs.

Miscellaneous

for: She was named for her   from: You cannot distin-
      aunt.   guish John from
      He is small for his age.   Jim.

---

2. USES OF PREPOSITIONS AFTER CERTAIN VERBS

account for	hear of
agree on (something)	insist on
agree with (someone)	invite (someone) to
apologize to	laugh at
approve of	listen for
argue with (someone)	listen to
ask for	look at
believe in	look for
belong to	look forward to
blame (someone) for (something)	object to
blame (something) on (someone)	plan on
borrow from	provide for
call on	provide with
care for	recover from
compliment (someone) on	remind (someone) of
consent to	see about
consist of	substitute for
convince (someone) of (something)	talk about
decide on	talk of
depend on	think about
get rid of	think of
hear about	wait for
hear from	wait on (meaning *serve*)

3. USES OF PREPOSITIONS WITH CERTAIN ADJECTIVES AND IN IDIOMATIC EXPRESSIONS

in accordance with
according to
accustomed to
angry about (something)
angry at (someone); or angry with (someone)
based on
capable of
composed of
content with
different from
disappointed in

due to
followed by
fond of
independent of
interested in
limited to
married to
proud of
in regard to
have respect for
similar to
tired of

D. Subordinators and Conjunctions

1. MARKERS OF SUBORDINATE CLAUSES

Time	Place	Condition	Cause
after	where	although	as
as	wheresoever	except that	because
as soon as	wherever	if	for
before		in case	lest
now that		only	in that
once	**Contrast**	provided that	why
since	whereas	unless	since
until (till)		whether	
when			**Purpose**
whenever	**Comparison**	**Manner**	so that
while	as though	how	
	than		

2. PAIRED CONJUNCTIONS

either . . . or	You can *either* go *or* stay. *Either* you go *or* I go.
neither . . . nor	*Neither* what he says *nor* what he does is becoming to a gentleman.
both . . . and	I like *both* what he has done *and* what he plans to do.
whether . . . or	*Whether* happy *or* sad, John is pleasant and courteous.
	Whether I go *or* I stay depends upon the news we get about Mother's health.
now . . . now (then, again)	He is *now* excited, *now* depressed.
rather . . . than	I would *rather* go to the tropics *than* trek to the North Pole.

Note the word order in the sentence patterns marked by the following paired conjunctions:

as . . . so	*As* the twig is bent, *so* is the tree inclined.
not only . . . but (but also, but . . . too)	*Not only* did my parents give him encouragement, *but* they gave him money too.
neither . . . nor	*Neither* can I go *nor* can I stay.

3. USES OF SENTENCE CONNECTORS

Markers that indicate contrast of ideas

however
nevertheless
yet

I enjoy shopping in the city; *however (nevertheless, yet)*, I would not like to live there.

Markers that indicate addition of an idea

also
furthermore
likewise
too

Colorado is a fine place for a vacation; *also (furthermore, likewise, too)*, it is a good place to live.[a]

Markers that indicate a more forceful restatement of an idea

indeed

This is a fine place for a vacation; *indeed*, it is the best we have found yet.

Markers that introduce clauses of result

consequently
hence
therefore
thus

He asked me to go; *therefore (consequently, hence, thus, so)*, I went.[b]

Markers that indicate time sequence

afterward(s)

First we went shopping; *afterward* we went to a play.

later on

Early in the evening we listened to music; *later on* we danced.

hereafter

Up to this time your assignments have been easy; *hereafter* they will be more difficult.[c]

thereafter

The accident occurred last year; *thereafter* he was more careful.[c]

thereupon

The teacher left the room; *thereupon* the students began to talk.

[a] *Also* and *too* are usually used at the end of a clause.

[b] *Consequently* and *therefore* are more used in writing than in speaking, and they are in more common use than *hence* and *thus*.

[c] Note the time relations expressed by *hereafter* and *thereafter,* as indicated by the forms of the verbs.

II. Conventions in the Mechanics of Writing

A. *Rules for Punctuation*

The general purpose of punctuation is to help make ideas clear to the reader. Use punctuation only when there is good reason for its use. Avoid overpunctuation, particularly the indiscriminate use of commas. Here are the standard rules.

▶ Period (.)

1. A period signals the end of each sentence pattern that expresses a statement or a command. Do not place a period after a group of words, no matter how long, that is not a sentence pattern.
2. A period is used after abbreviations.

Street: St.	Mister: Mr.	et cetera: etc.
Doctor: Dr.	January: Jan.	(and so forth)

▶ Question Mark (?)

1. A question mark is used after a question, even though the question may be phrased as a statement.

   How did he do it?
   He did?

2. Do not use a question mark after an indirect question, a request, or an included clause introduced by an interrogative word.

He asked me how I did it.
Please give me the book.
I wonder why she said that.

▶ Comma (,)

1. A comma is used between two sentence patterns joined by *and, but, or, for, nor,* and *so* unless these patterns are very short.

   I would like to accept your invitation, but I shall be out of town on that date.
   There was nothing more that we could do, so we went home.

2. A comma is used between items in a series. The series may be composed of single words, phrases, or clauses.

   The professor gave a long, dull, but exceedingly learned lecture.
   We looked in the house, in the garden, in the barn, and in the attic, but we could not find the cat.

3. A comma is used after word groups acting as modifiers if these word groups begin a sentence. Long word groups used as modifiers often occur at the beginning of a sentence pattern. Such elements are separated from the rest of the sentence by a comma.

   When we finally got home after our long trip, we felt as though we had never been away.
   Unused to so much excitement, the child fell asleep.

4. A comma is used around interrupting or parenthetical elements in a sentence. Following are common interrupting elements:
   a. Nonrestrictrive constructions (word groups giving information about a noun that has already been identified).

   This book, which I hope you will read soon, gives a complete account of that important event.
   The soldiers, weary and footsore, straggled up the road.

   b. Expressions like *I think.*

   This is, I believe, the first time such a thing has ever happened here.

5. A comma is used in the following conventional places:
   a. In dates.

   January 17, 1968

   b. In addresses.

   1044 High Street, New York City, New York

   c. After the name of a state when a city and state are mentioned together within a sentence.

   New Orleans, Louisiana, is my hometown.

   d. In figures, to separate thousands.

   1,000 (or 1000)
   10,000
   15,500,000

   e. With nouns in direct address.

   Look, John!
   Yes, Mary, it is.

   f. With titles and degrees.

   John Jones, M.D., LL.D.
   John Jones, Captain of the Guard

   g. After the salutation in informal letters.

   Dear Mother,

   h. After the complementary close in letters.

   Sincerely yours,
   Yours very truly,

   i. With phrases introducing direct quotations.

   William said, "Come here."
   "I don't know," Lee said, "of a better place."

   j. To separate the sentence connectors *therefore, consequently, however,* and so on, from the rest of the clause in which they occur.

Jim likes Pete; however, I do not care for him.
Jim likes Pete; I, however, do not care for him.
Jim likes Pete; I do not care for him, however.

Note the semicolon to mark the end of the sentence pattern.

▶ Semicolon (;)

1. Use a semicolon between sentence patterns (two main clauses) that are closely connected in idea.

   a. When the two patterns are not joined by any connective.

   That is a good idea; I think we can use it.

   b. When the two patterns are joined by a sentence connector.

   The job was difficult; however, he did it well.

   c. When the two patterns are joined by a conjunction (*and, but,* etc.), but each sentence pattern contains considerable internal punctuation.

   I have not forgotten Washington, New York, San Francisco, and Las Vegas; nor have I forgotten my trips to Chicago, Los Angeles, and Spokane.

2. Use a semicolon to separate word groups that contain commas within them.

   For officers we elected Jim Brown, the banker, as president; Cliff Burns, superintendent of schools, as vice president; Mark Harmon, the well-known lawyer, as secretary; and Steve Granger, an officer of the milling company, as treasurer.

▶ Colon (:)

Whereas a semicolon separates, a colon introduces or directs attention to what is to follow.

1. A colon is used between two sentence patterns when the second pattern explains, restates, or implies the first.

   They raised the tuition for one reason only: they could not operate on the current revenue.

2. A colon is used after a sentence pattern when an enumeration or an explanation is to follow.

There are three ways to get there: by car, by bus, or by plane.

3. A colon is used in certain conventional places:
   a. After the salutation in a formal letter.

   Dear Mr. Jackson:

   b. Between hours and minutes expressed in figures.

   12:00
   2:45

   c. Preceding long quoted passages.

► **Dash (—)**

1. A dash marks a more abrupt break in thought than a comma. It is used to indicate an abrupt turn of idea, and often parenthetical material.

The students at this university—at least the ones that I have talked to—seem to have a sound knowledge of the subject.

2. A dash is used to emphasize a phrase or to make it dramatic.

There is only one way to describe it—terrible!

► **Exclamation Point (!)**

An exclamation point is used after a forceful or emotional statement, whether it is a complete sentence pattern or not.

Look out!
How wonderful!

► **Quotation Marks (". . .") or ('. . .')**

Quotation marks are always used in pairs. Both elements in the pair are placed above the line, as illustrated.

1. Double quotation marks are used to enclose direct quotations—the actual words of a given speaker or writer.

   He said, "I believe this is a good solution to the problem."

2. Double quotation marks are used for short quotations from writers. However, long quotations are generally indented and single-spaced on the typewriter, but not enclosed in quotation marks.

3. Single quotation marks are used to mark a quotation within a quotation.

   The boy replied, "My father always told me, 'John, don't do anything hastily.' "

4. Double quotation marks are used within sentences to indicate the titles of works of art, short musical compositions and short poems, the chapters of a book, and so on.

   Leonardo da Vinci's "Mona Lisa"
   Edvard Grieg's "Piano Concerto in A Minor"

5. Double quotation marks are used to indicate a word used as an example in a sentence rather than for its meaning. Some writers prefer underscoring or italicizing such words.

   "Warbling" is a musical word.
   Look up the meaning of *isotope*.

6. Double quotation marks are used to indicate that a term is used by a particular person or group for a particular purpose. The writer may not agree with this use of the term, and shows it by his use of quotation marks.

   His "mechanical invention," like most of his other bright ideas, did not work.

▶ **Parentheses ( )**

1. Parentheses are used for explanatory remarks.
2. Parentheses are used around figures and letters to enumerate points in outlines or in a body of written material.

Metaphors (suggested comparisons) are frequently used in poetry.

You must try to (1) finish the project and (2) finish it on time.

▶ Brackets [ ]

Brackets are used to enclose explanations in material quoted from other writers. The material within brackets is clearly not the words of the quoted writer.

"He [the American Indian] has left his stamp upon America."

▶ Ellipsis (. . .)

Three spaced periods indicate that one or more words have been omitted from quoted material. If the omission occurs at the end of a sentence, use three spaced periods to indicate the omission and follow them by another period to end the sentence.

▶ Apostrophe (')

1. An apostrophe is used in contractions. (Contractions are not generally favored in formal writing.)

   hasn't   didn't   o'clock   it's (it is)

2. An apostrophe is used in plurals of letters and figures.

   to's   i's   the 1400's

3. An apostrophe is used to indicate possession. In a plural word, and in a singular word of two or more syllables ending in –*s*, no extra *s* is added.

   Susan's coat   the children's coats
   the boy's coat   the boys' coats
   James's hat   Diogenes' lantern

4. An apostrophe is not used with *its, my, his,* and other posessive forms of pronouns.

▶ Underlining

Underlining in typewriting or handwriting serves the same purpose as italics in printed material. These are the uses of underlining.

1. Underline titles of books, plays, magazines, newspapers, long musical scores, and so on.

Why We Behave like Americans   *My Fair Lady*
Harper's Magazine   *The New York Times*
      Beethoven's *Ninth Symphony*

2. Underline words used as words.

Say *and* with emphasis.

3. Underline words from foreign languages when used in English sentences.

ad hoc

sine qua non

persona non grata

4. Underline words for emphasis. Reserve this for rare occasions, however.

B. Rules for Capitalization

1. The first word of a sentence should be capitalized. The first word of a direct quotation within a sentence is capitalized if the quotation is itself a complete sentence.
2. Capitalize proper names.
   a. People—their names and titles (see g, which follows).
   b. Geographical places and the names of the people who live in these places.

   London, Londoners   India, Indians

   c. Languages and the names of school subjects deriving from languages.

   Italian   German   Portuguese   Japanese

d. Days of the week, months of the year, and holidays, but not generally the names of centuries and not the names of the seasons.

Sunday	Christmas	the fifteenth
January	summer	century

e. Names of structures, bridges, highways, and ships.

the Montauk Highway	Rockefeller Center
Brooklyn Bridge	the S.S. *Queen Mary*

f. Titles of school courses, but not the simple identification of a course.

Speech 495	speech
Biology 111	biology
Survey of English Literature	literature

g. Titles and words showing family relationships when with proper names, in direct address, and in direct reference without a noun marker.

President Roosevelt	Doctor Jones	Aunt Mary

Good morning, Grandfather.
I received a letter from Mother.

but:

I visited the doctor today.
Which professor teaches English?
He received a letter from his mother.

h. Important words (usually, all words except *a, the,* conjunctions, and prepositions of four letters or fewer when not at the beginning) in titles of books, magazines, newspapers, plays, and so on.

The Second Tree from the Corner
Art and Literary Digest
Training in Business and Industry

i. Racial, religious, and political groups.

Negroes	Methodists	Democrats

j. Names of historical events and documents.

the French Revolution　　the Constitution

k. Names of organizations.

the Red Cross　　Delta Tau Delta

l. Words that refer to the deity.

Jehovah	Him	His name
God	Who	Christ

m. The pronoun *I*.
n. Words that refer to the whole or parts of a body of land or water.

the Western Hemisphere	the Grand Banks
the Indian Ocean	the South Pacific
the South (of the U.S.)	Western Europe

C. Forms for Acknowledging Borrowed Material and Ideas

▶ **Footnotes**

In footnotes give the author's name, the title of the book or article, the edition, the place of publication, the publisher, the date of publication, and the page number of the material referred to. Use the following examples as models for punctuation, and punctuate consistently and exactly.

[1] Alfred Korzybski, *Science and Sanity,* 4th ed. (Clinton, Mass.: Colonial Press, 1973), p. 35.
[2] Muriel Sibell Wolle, *Stampede to Timberline,* rev. ed. (Chicago: Swallow Press, 1974), p. 21.
[3] Octavio Paz, *Conjunctions and Disjunctions,* trans. Helen R. Lane (New York: Viking, 1974), p. 14.
[4] Harold Goodglass and Sheila Blumstein, *Psycholinguistics and Aphasia* (Baltimore: Johns Hopkins University Press, 1973), p. 167.

⁵ W. Ashton Ellis, *Correspondence of Wagner and Liszt,* vol. 1, 2nd rev. ed., trans. Francis Hueffer (New York: Vienna House, 1973), p. 253.

⁶ "Cities Where Business Is Best," *U.S. News and World Report,* vol. 77, no. 15 (October 7, 1974), 78–81.

⁷ "Airship," *Encyclopedia Britannica,* I, 73.

▶ Bibliography

List bibliographical items in alphabetical order by the author's last name, or by the first important word of the title if no author is given (*A* and *The* are not counted).

Fries, Charles C. *The Structure of English.* New York: Harcourt Brace Jovanovich, 1952, pp. 240–255.

Information Please Almanac, 1947–1958. Garden City, N.Y.: Doubleday, 1947. 2 vols.

Leonard, George B. "Language and Reality," *Harper's Magazine,* vol. 249, no. 1494 (November 1974), 46–52.

Vidal, Gore. *Burr.* New York: Random House, 1973, pp. 285–359.

D. *Abbreviations*

Here are common abbreviations used in writing, with an explanation of their meaning and suggestions for their use. Note that some abbreviations derived from Latin terms are not set in italics.

ed.—edition, editor, edited by

e.g. (*exempli gratia*)—"for example"

ibid. (*ibidem*)—"in the same place" as the immediately preceding reference. If the page reference is not the same, then use: *ibid.,* p. 25.

i.e. (*id est*)—"that is"

loc. cit. (*loco citato*)—"in the place cited." Suppose reference has been made to the book *Excellence* by John Gardner. Then reference is made to works by Smith, Eiseley, and Jones. Following this is a reference to the work already referred to by Gardner. The reference would look like this: Gardner, *loc. cit.*

op. cit. (opere citato)—"in the work cited." Suppose a reference has been made to something on page 12 of Gardner's *Excellence,* and then one or more references are made to other works. Later you wish to refer to another passage in Gardner's book. The entry might look like this: Gardner, *op. cit.,* p. 56.

p.—page

pp.—pages

rev. ed.—revised edition

tr., trans.—translator, translated by

vol. (vols.)—volume (volumes)

Index

A, an, 19–24
   summary of uses, 21
Abbreviations, 259–260
Absolute construction, 84
Addition, markers to indicate, 248
Adjectival clauses, 66–69, 122
Adjectives
   comparative degree of, 56–57
   as complements, 6, 7
   describing with, 56
   following noun, 57–58
   as modifiers of nouns, 56–57
   as objective complements, 6
   order preceding noun, 57–58
   position of, 57–58
   with prepositional phrases, 38
   qualifiers of, 57; *enough* as
      qualifier, 57
   as subjective complement, 6–7
"Adventure on the Colorado," 18–19
Adverbial clauses, 82–84
   reduction of, 83–84
Adverbial phrases, 122–123, 243–245
   expressing association, 245
   expressing manner, 244
   expressing means or agent, 244
   expressing place or direction, 243

expressing purpose, 245
expressing quantity, 244
expressing state or condition, 244
expressing time, 243
Adverbs
   as complements, 7
   formation of, 50
   as modifiers of sentences, 49
   as modifiers of verbs, 47–51
   most common uses of, 47–48
   placement of, 48–50
   in sentence patterns, 4–5, 7
   of time as organizational device,
      53, 144–146
   in two-word verbs, 36–37
Affirmative sentence patterns. *See*
   Sentence patterns
Agreement, subject–verb, 8
"Alexander of Macedon," 129
"The American Frontier," 170–171
"Animal Wisdom," 137–138
"The Antarctic: Home of the
   Wind," 146–147
Appositives, 68, 122
"The Arab World," 55–66

Arranging main points. *See*
　　Selecting and arranging main
　　points
Articles, 19–25
Assertions, 126
　　examples of, 126, 127
　　present tense with, 30
　　use of in compositions, 126, 127
"At the Airport," 73–74
Attitudes, expression of, with
　　modals. *See* Modal auxiliaries
Authority, as method of
　　development, 139–140

Be
　　expressing future, 35, 235, 236,
　　　242
　　in past continuous, 33–34
　　in passive voice, 60–63
　　in present continuous, 32–33
　　sentence patterns with, 7;
　　　affirmative, 7; interrogative,
　　　12; negative, 8; variations of,
　　　15–16
Be about to, 242
Becker, Carl, 171
Bibliography, form of, 259
Burdick, Eugene, 126

Calhoun, John C., 66
"California Gold," 87–88
Can + v, 92, 238
Capitalization, rules for, 256–258
Carson, Rachel, 15–16
Cause-effect order, 176–180
"The Changing Sea," 15–16
"The Charisma of the Golden Gate
　　Bridge," 126
Chronological order, 144–146
Ciafardoni, Thomas, 40
"Civilization's Debt to Books," 4
Classification. *See* Topical order
Clauses
　　conditional, 93, 238–239
　　coordinate, 85, 250, 252–253
　　as modifiers of nouns, 66–69, 122
　　as modifiers of sentences, 82
　　as modifiers of verbs, 82–84
　　as nouns, 80–81
　　reduced to infinitives, 70
　　reduced to participial
　　　constructions, 70–74

with relative pronouns, 66–69
restrictive and nonrestrictive,
　　68–69
Collier's, 130
Combining sentence patterns
　　by conjunctions, 85, 247
　　by sentence connectors, 85–88
Comparative forms of adjectives,
　　56–57
Comparison, as rhetorical device,
　　166–168
Complement
　　adjective, 6–7
　　adverb, 7
　　with *be,* 7
　　objective, 6
　　subjective, 6–7
Composition assignments
　　definition, 112, 174
　　description, 63–64
　　essay examination answer,
　　　200–201
　　evaluative essay, 195
　　expository, 28, 39, 75, 89, 99, 123,
　　　143, 175, 185–186
　　inductive organization in, 195
　　problem-solving sequence of,
　　　185–187
　　process, 160–161
　　requiring library research, 225
　　spatial arrangement in, 63–64
　　time arrangement in, 53, 161
Composition
　　central idea of, 117–118. *See also*
　　　Thesis sentence
　　choosing a subject of, 113–119
　　conclusion of, 119
　　developing ideas in, 125–143
　　introduction to, 119
　　limiting subject of, 114, 115
　　organizing of, 144–201. *See also*
　　　Organizational patterns
　　outlining of, 179, 181–185
　　point of view in, 114, 115–117
　　purpose in, 114
　　stating the subject of, 119–121
　　thesis sentence, statement of. *See*
　　　Thesis sentence
　　transitional devices in, 119
Comparison, 97

Conclusions
  in composition, 119
  in logic, 126, 127
  support of, 125–140
Conditional sentences, 93
Conjecture, 93
Conjunctions, 85, 240
  paired, 247
Connectors, sentence, 85, 248
Continuous forms of verbs, 22–23,
  32, 33–34, 44–45, 47
Contrast
  markers indicating, 94, 248
  as rhetorical method, 168–171
Coordination, structures of, 15, 85,
  250, 252–253
Could + v, 92, 93, 94, 238
Count nouns, 19–21
Cultures, view of time by different,
  29–30
Customs and culture, 29–30

Debenham, Frank, 146
Deductive order, as rhetorical device, 188–191
Deductive reasoning, 109–110, 111
  defined, 109
  examples of, 109
Definition, 112, 162–166, 174
  composition assignment, 112, 174
"Definition of a Paragraph,"
  164–166
"Definition of Psychoanalysis," 163
Description
  composition assignment, 63–64
  with the passive, 60–61
Désirée, 130
Details, use of as rhetorical device,
  127–130
Developing ideas
  by authority, 139–140
  by comparison, 166–168
  by definition, 162–166
  by details, 127–130
  by examples, 7–8, 135–136
  by explanation, 171–173
  by facts, 130–131
  by figures, 131–134
  by illustration, 137–138
  by quotation from authority,
   139–141
  by statistics, 134–135

rationale for, 125–126
  by restatement, 173–174
Diez, Ernest, 59–60
"Differences in the Development of
  Writing and Speech in the
  Individual," 168–170
Direct object, 5–7, 9–10
Don't have to + v, 93

Eisenhower, Dwight, 65
el Hafez, Mousa, 115
Elliptical construction, 83–84
Emerson, Ralph Waldo, 86–87
Enough, placement of, 57
Essay examinations, writing answers
  to, 197–200
Evaluative essay, techniques of
  writing, 195–197
"Evenings with Music," 167
Ewen, David, 139
Examinations, writing, 197–200
Examples, development by, 7–8,
  135–136
Explanation, as rhetorical device,
  171–173
Expository composition assignments,
  28, 39, 75, 89, 99, 123, 143,
  175, 185–186

Facts, as rhetorical method,
  130–131, 140
Few, a few, 26–27
Figures, as rhetorical method,
  131–134, 141
Flag, U.S., 14
Footnoting, 210–217, 258–259
"For and Against Heroes," 218–223
Freud, Sigmund, 163
Future time, expressions of, 35–36,
  235, 236, 240, 242

"A General Introduction to
  Psychoanalysis," 163
Generalizations
  defined, 109
  rationale for, 109
Gerunds, 77–79
Get to + v, 235
Going to + v, 35, 235
Golden Gate Bridge, 126, 128
Grand Canyon, 18–19

Hartley, Fred A., Jr., 132
Have to + v, 93, 241, 242
"Hawaii," 68–69
Hawkes, Albert, 136
Hawthorne, Nathaniel, 87
Henry, Joseph, 66
"History," 171
Hook, J. N., 191
Hoover, Herbert, 65
"How Different Cultures View
    Time," 29–30
Hypothetical statements, 93

If, sentences with, 93
Illustration, as rhetorical method,
    137–138, 141
Indirect object, 5
Inductive order, as rhetorical device,
    191–195
  composition assignment, 195
Inductive reasoning, defined, 109
Inference, 95
Infinitives and infinitive
    constructions, 96–98
  as adverbials, 96
  as complements of adjectives, 96
  to express purpose, 96
  as modifiers of nouns, 70–71,
    72–73
  as nouns, 77–79, 80–81
  used with adjectives, 96–97, 98
In the Ancient Worlds of Asia,
    59–60
"The Influence of the American
    Frontier," 176–179
"The Influence of the American
    Indian on American Culture,"
    149–151
Interrogative patterns. *See* Question
    patterns
Intransitive verb, 5
"An Intriguing Legacy," 130–131
Introductions to essays, 119
It
  as sentence filler, 13–14, 96–99
  sentence pattern with, 13–14

Jefferson, Thomas, 65

Kennedy, John, 58, 151
Kreisler, Fritz, 139

Lamb, Harold, 129
"Language and Culture," 76–77
Lapp language, 76–77
Leopold, Aldo, 192, 194
Library research paper
  composition assignment, 225
  crediting sources, 216–218, 258
  finding material, 203–206
  how to write, 202–224
  integrating material, 211–215
  taking notes, 207–211
"Linguistic Change," 191
Linking verb, 6
"Listen to the Mocking Words," 139
Literary work, evaluation of, 197
Little, a little, 26
*The Lost Letters of Marie-Louise
    to Napoleon,* 130–131

McCrimmon, James, 98
"Magnanimity," 189–190
Marie-Louise, 130–131
"Mark Twain and the Mississippi,"
    205–206
Markers
  of nouns, 19–28
  of sequence of tenses, 85–88, 94,
    248
  of subordinate clauses, 66–68,
    81–85, 246
Mathews, E. G., 191
May + v, 92, 239
"Mesa Verde," 90–91
Might + v, 92, 235, 239
Modal auxiliaries, 91–96, 235–242
Modifiers
  of adjectives and adverbs. *See*
    Qualifiers
  of nouns, adjectival clauses as,
    66–69; adjectives as, 56–59;
    adverbial clauses as, 82–84;
    adverbial phrases as, 122–123,
    243–245; appositives as, 68,
    122; order in a series, 57–58;
    verbal constructions as, 69–74,
    142–143
  prepositional phrases, 38–39, 122,
    243–245
  of sentences, 49
  of verbs, 47–51, 122–123, 243–245
  verb forms as, 69–74

Must + v, 93, 95, 241
   compared with *have to,* 93, 241
   contrasted with *should,* 92, 95
   lack of past tense of, 241
Must not + v, 93, 242
"My Absent-Minded Friends," 46
"My Point of View Toward Home,"
   115–117

Napoleon, 130–131
Nida, Eugene, 30
Nonrestrictive clauses, 66–69
Noun clauses, 80–81
Nouns
   count, 19–21
   markers of, 19–28; *a, the,* 19–25;
     other, 25–29
   non-count, 19–21; charts of,
     230–232; definitized, 20–21
   plurals of, regular, 229; irregular,
     229–230
   as subject of infinitive, 79
Nurredin, Numati, 120

Object
   direct, 5–7, 9–10
   indirect, 5
Objective complement, 6
"The Old and the New," 55–56
Organizational patterns, 144–152,
   176–185, 188–195
   cause-effect, 176–180
   deductive, 188–191
   inductive, 191–195
   problem-solution, 180–185
   space, 146–148
   time, 144–146
   topical, 148–152
"Orientation Program," 62
Ought to + v, 92, 93, 94
Outlining, 152–160
   arrangement of main points,
     152–153
   developmental material in,
     155–157
   examples of, 153–154, 156–157,
     179, 180–181
   forms and uses, 154–155
   master plan for, 155
   questions about, 155, 157–158
   specific purpose in, 155, 156

supporting material in, 155–157
thesis sentence in, 155

Paired conjunctions, 247
Paragraph, definition of, 164–166
Paragraph composition assignments
   description, 17, 34, 58, 61–62
   exposition, 7, 8, 9, 10, 11, 12,
     14, 23, 31–32, 35–36, 38, 44–45,
     59, 78–81, 93
   narration, 45–46
   progression in time, 53
   using contrast, 11
   using examples, 94, 95
   using questions, 12
Parallel structure, 16
Parrish, W. N., 173
Participles
   as modifiers of nouns, 70–72
   with noun subjects, 79
   as part of verb phrase, 32–34,
     41–47
Passive voice, 60–63. *See also* Verbs
Past participles
   as modifiers of nouns, 70–72
   as part of the verb, 41–43, 45–46
Past perfect, 45–46
   continuous, 47
Past tense, 33
   continuous, 33–34
Patterning ideas, 164
Patterns of arrangement of
   expository material, 144–152,
     176–185, 188–195. *See also*
     Organizational patterns
Philip of Macedon, 129
Plurals of nouns, 229, 230
Possessive, use of apostrophe to
   denote, 255
Premise, major and minor, 109
Prepositions
   in adverbial phrases, 243–245
   determined by preceding
     adjective, 38, 246
   determined by preceding verb, 38,
     245
   in idiomatic expressions, 246
Present continuous, 22–23
Present participles
   as modifiers of nouns, 70–72
   as part of the verb, 32–33, 33–34

Present perfect, 41–43
  continuous, 44–45
Present tense, 8, 30–32
Principal parts of irregular verbs, 232–233
Problem-solution order as rhetorical device, 180–187
  composition assignment, 185–187
Process, composition assignment describing, 160–161
Pronouns
  personal, 26
  relative, 66–69
  as subject of infinitive, 79
Punctuation
  apostrophe, 255
  brackets, 255
  colon, 252–253
  comma, 250–252
  of coordinate clauses, 250, 252
  dash, 253
  ellipsis, 255
  exclamation point, 253
  in letter, 251, 253
  of noun plus modifiers, 250
  parentheses, 254–255
  period, 249
  question mark, 249
  quotation marks, 253–254
  semicolon, 252
  between sentence patterns, 250, 252
  of subordinate clauses, 250
  underlining, 256
Purpose, in composition, 114, 115

Qualifiers, of adjectives, 57
"Qualities of a Leader," 58
Questions
  difference between *shall* and *will* in, 35–36, 236
  word order in, 12
Quotation
  from authority, as rhetorical method, 139–140, 141
  direct, 46, 253–254
  indirect, verb forms in, 46

Reasoning
  conclusion in, 109–111
  deductive, 109, 110–111

generalizations, 109
  inductive, 109
  major premise, 109
  minor premise, 109
Relative clauses as modifiers, 66–69
Relative pronouns
  introducing clauses modifying nouns, 66–69
  omission of, 67
Repetition of sentence elements, 16
Reported speech, 46
Requests, 36, 236, 237
Research writing. *See* Library research paper
Restatement
  markers to indicate, 248
  as rhetorical device, 173–174
Restrictive clause, 68–69, 122
Result
  clauses of, 88
  markers of, 88, 248
Rhetoric
  defined, 103–104
  history of, 104
  need for, 104, 110
  organization in, defined, 105–106
  rationale for the study of, 105–106, 109–110
"Rhetoric Across Cultures," 108–111
"Rhetoric: What Is It and Why Study It?" 103–106
Rhetorical devices
  arrangement of main points, 144–145, 146, 152–153, 179, 181–185
  development of ideas, defined, 106
  methods of development. *See* Developing ideas
  organizational patterns. *See* Organizational patterns
Robinson, James Harvey, 159

Scientific research, techniques for writing, 196
Scott, Sir Walter, 189
The Sea Around Us, 15
Selecting and arranging main points, 152–153
Sentence connectors, 85–88, 248
  to show addition, 248
  to show contrast, 248
  to show restatement, 248

Sentence connectors (*Continued*)
  to show result, 248
  to show time sequence, 248
Sentence modifiers, 49
Sentence patterns
  affirmative, 5–6
  basic elements in, 5–7
  with *be*, 7
  charted and explained, 5–7
  combining, 73–74
  conditional, 93
  conjunctions combining, 85, 246
  elliptical, 83–84
  identification of, 71, 83
  interrogative, 12
  interrupting elements in, 250
  inverted order in, 96–97
  modification patterns within. *See*
    Modifiers
  negative patterns, 8
  punctuation between, 7–12, 95,
    96
  question patterns, 12
  relating, 173, 246–248
  repetition of elements in, 16
  sequencing, 85–88, 248
  sequencing of tenses in, 94, 248
  there and *it* as starters, 13–14,
    96–97
  word order in, 7
Shall + v, 35–36, 240
Should + v, 92, 93, 95, 235, 240
  contrasted with *must*, 92
  contrasted with *shall*, 92
Skolsky, Syd, 167
Smith, Bradford, 170
Smithson, James, 65–66
Smithsonian Institution, 65–66
Snow, C. P., 189
So, so that, 88
Some
  contrasted with *any*, 26
  meanings of, 26
"Some Animal and Insect Traits,"
  69–70
Spatial
  composition assignments, 63–64
  organization, 63–64, 73–74,
    146–148
Specific details, as rhetorical
  method, 127–130

Speech, evaluation of, 197
Statistics, as rhetorical method,
  134–135
Stewart, Desmond, 55
Subject of essay
  choosing, 113–119
  limiting, 114–115
  stating, 119
Subject of infinitive, 79, 234
Subordinate clauses, 81–82
Subordinators, 81–85, 246
"Success at an Early Age," 136
Supporting material, 125–140

Tenses. *See* Verbs
Testimony (quotation from
  authority), 139–140, 141
That, as simple clause marker, 67,
  80
The, 19–25
  with count nouns, 20–21
  with non-count nouns, 19–21
There, sentence patterns with, 7,
  13–14
Thesis sentence, 27, 39, 75, 111–112,
  117, 119, 121, 123–124, 145,
  146, 147, 152, 153, 154, 155,
  156, 159, 179, 181–182,
  183–185, 205
  defined, 27
"Thinking Like a Mountain,"
  192–194
This, that, these, those, 26
Thoreau, Henry David, 86–87
"Those Inventive Americans," 133
"Thought and Language," 168
"The Throne Room," 59–60
Time
  adverbials to express, 4–16
  adverbs to express, 4–16
  order, as rhetorical pattern,
    144–146; composition
    assignment, 53, 161
  sequence markers of, 4–16, 248
  verbs to express, 32–36
Time magazine, 218–223
To + v. *See* Infinitives and infinitive
  constructions
Tolstoi, Lev Nikolaevich, 189–190
Too
  position of, 97
  as qualifier, 97

Topic sentence, 7, 14, 23, 27, 28, 31, 34, 44, 53, 88, 93, 124, 140
defined, 27
Topical order, 148–152
Transitional devices, 85–88, 108, 145, 147, 166
Transitive verb, 5
Turgenev, Ivan Sergevich, 189–190
Two-word verbs, 36–37
Tzeltal Indians, 76–77

"Undersea Museums," 40–41
"An Unusual Bequest," 65–66

Verbals. *See also* Infinitives and infinitive constructions; Participles
as modifiers of noun, 70–74, 77
as nouns, 77–79, 80–81
types of verbs followed by, 234–235
as verb elements, 32, 33
Verbs
controlling prepositions, 245
followed by verbals, 88; chart of, 234
forms of, in conditional sentences, 93
future, 35
governing prepositions, 38, 245
intransitive, 5
irregular forms of, 232–233
linking, 6, 11
modal auxiliaries, 235–242
modifiers of. *See* Adverbial clauses; Adverbial phrases; Adverbs
passive voice, 60–63; contrasted with active, 61; defined, 63;

proper use of, 61; weakness of, 61
past perfect, 45–46; continuous form of, 47; in reported speech, 46
past tense, 33; continuous form of, 33–34
present perfect, 41–43; continuous form of, 44–45
present tense, 8, 30–31; continuous form of, 32–33
sequence of tenses, 94
simple form of, use after selected verbs, 235. *See also* Past tense; Present tense
transitive, 5
two-word, 36
Vergara, William C., 51
"The View from Golden Gate Bridge," 128
Voice, active and passive, 60–63
"The Voices of the Strings," 167
Vygotsky, Lev, 168, 170

Washington, George, 65
"Weathermaking," 51
Wechsberg, Joseph, 140
What, in noun clauses, 80
"What Home Means to Me," 120–124
"Why We Behave Like Americans," 170
Will + v, 35–36, 92, 236, 240
Winterowd, W. Ross, 165
Word order in basic sentences, 5–9, 11–14
Would + v, 92, 93, 94, 235, 237
"The Wright Brothers' First Airplane Flight," 133–134